CW01459231

6 San Lorenzo fuori le Mura
7 Santa Maria in Cosmedin
8 Santa Maria in Trastevere
9 San Nicola in Carcere
10 Santa Sabina
11 Santo Stefano Rotondo

1 Sant'Adriano
2 San Bartolomeo all'Isola
3 San Benedetto in Piscinula
4 Santa Bibiana
5 Santi Cosma e Damiano
6 San Crisogono
7 San Giovanni in Laterano
   (the Lateran Basilica)
8 San Giovanni a Porta Latina
9 Santi Giovanni e Paolo
10 San Lorenzo in Miranda
11 Santa Maria degli Angeli
12 Santa Maria Antiqua
13 Santa Maria in Aracoeli
14 Santa Maria in Domnica
15 Santa Maria Egiziaca
16 Santa Maria Maggiore
17 Santa Maria Rotonda
18 San Martino ai Monti
19 Santi Nereo e Achilleo
20 San Paolo fuori le Mura
21 St Peter's (San Pietro)
22 San Pietro in Vincoli
23 Santa Prassede
24 Santa Prisca
25 Santa Pudenziana
26 Santi Quattro Coronati
27 San Saba
28 Sancta Sanctorum

MH

MARIA FABRICIUS HANSEN

THE SPOLIA CHURCHES OF ROME

Recycling Antiquity in the Middle Ages

*Translated from the Danish
by Barbara J. Haveland*

AARHUS UNIVERSITY PRESS

Glossary

Architectural terms and the names of different types of stone listed in the glossary (p. 238) or the guide to materials (p. 243) are given in italics the first time they are mentioned in the introductory chapters or the descriptions of churches.

Numbering

[1] Numbers in square brackets refer to illustrations.

❶ Numbers in red circles refer to the eleven selected churches, each described in a separate chapter.

❶ Numbers in blue circles refer to the "Other noteworthy spolia churches" listed at the end of this book, in the section on Practical Information.

The red and blue numbers also indicate the locations of churches on the maps at the front and back of the book.

Recycling Antiquity

Selected spolia churches

Practical Information

...IVIVS
...RTHOPVS
...T CONIVGI

Recycling
Antiquity

...CωCA

OCEIΛE

ΛλUOΓ

NZEYΓ

ΛEΞATO

ACAΓNC

Introduction

ROME IS BUILT on the past. There can hardly be any other city in the world whose history can so readily be traced: through the wealth of physical reminders still to be found there. A whole succession of different periods – the Middle Ages, the Renaissance, the Baroque era and all the others in between, right up to the present day – have left their mark on 'the Eternal City'. And of course beneath all the other layers, like a keynote, lies Ancient Rome. As the capital of a vast empire, Ancient Rome had a name and a standing which, in all the centuries since then, have been a source of admiration and inspiration.

To this day, almost everywhere you go in the centre of Rome or in the surrounding area the vestiges of antiquity can still be seen. And not just in such famous buildings as the Colosseum or the Pantheon, impressive for their very size alone, or in the large areas of archaeological interest which are rather like historic parks, the Forum Romanum being the most renowned of these. In the streets, too, here a column built into a house, there a fountain constructed out of ancient elements chimes with the city's antique echo [1] [2] [3].

A particularly robust approach to Rome's antique past was taken in the Middle Ages, or rather: from Late Antiquity in the fourth century until around the thirteenth century. During this period people built quite literally both with and on antiquity, working as they did to a great extent with recycled materials (or recycling entire buildings, come to that) from ancient times, what are known as *spolia*: columns, marble panels, bricks – it was all there for the taking. There were times when buildings such as the Colosseum actually functioned as handy quarries full of prefabricated masonry.

The Latin word *spolium* originally meant the flayed skin of an animal, but in its plural form *spolia*, it came to denote different sorts of plunder – the booty of war, for example. This spolia eventually became the general term for architectural elements or pieces of sculpture taken from one site and reused in a different spot, often in a different way. The interesting thing for a visitor to Rome today is that in the Middle Ages no attempt was made to conceal this use of second-hand materials. Often, architectural elements from

1 Spolia columns on a street in Rome. Via Portico d'Ottavia.

quite different sources were combined in creative and unorthodox fashion, and the builders were not always so intent on getting the pieces to match in terms of size. Quite the contrary. They seem in fact to have favoured the idea of the various elements being as disparate and multifarious as possible ❼ [**84**].

To the visitor today these creative combinations of all sorts of materials and styles seem fascinating and instantly appealing – not to say downright entertaining. It can become something of a sport: going around the city and its buildings, hunting for recycled antiquities. Often these are to be found in churches. As an institution the church was a major force, culturally, economically and politically, and from the beginning of the fourth century (when Christianity became legal) it invested a great deal in its buildings which, as a result, house a rich variety of fine antique elements. As a visitor to Rome today you do however have to know what you are looking for in order to see it, so to speak. Over the centuries many of the churches have been 'modernized', with the addition of new chapels, altars, frescoes and so on which tend to smother the more discreet Medieval features. Often you have to consciously look for the variations in a colonnade in order to spot them and it takes a certain amount of training to be able to differentiate between the Medieval materials and later substitutions, alterations and modern restoration work. But the reward is that one leaves the church with a new sense of having listened to a long and fascinating story. The sort of story which only a building which has stood at the heart of European culture for so many politically and socially stormy and eventful centuries can tell. This book is intended, therefore, as a guide for those eager to get off the beaten track of mainstream tourism and explore the phenomenon of spolia in the Medieval churches of Rome.

The first section of this book is devoted to a discussion of spolia, their history, use, stylistic features and significance. The second section, a catalogue of sorts, contains more detailed descriptions and illustrations of eleven churches. These factual descriptions can be referred to when you are visiting a particular church and want to know what is what. They have therefore been written in such a way that they can be read separately and independently of the book's first half (so the reader will have to bear with me if I occasionally repeat myself). In the presentations of these selected churches you will find the basic information about the history of each building, together with descriptions of which antique architectural elements have been used in it and how. These eleven churches are particularly worth visiting because they represent different forms of architectural recycling from different periods of the Middle Ages – and, not least, because in its architectonic totality each one is quite unique, both from an aesthetic-artistic point of view and as a historic monument. Visit one or two churches a day on a standard week's holiday and you can gain a very good impression of the

2 Columns set into a house front. Via della Tribuna Campitelli.

3 Spolia columns in Via Santa Maria in Monticelli.

Medieval churches of Rome and their antique spoils. You don't even have to visit that many, though, since each church is in itself a sight worth seeing. Finally, in the last section of the book, you will find practical information and aids to further exploration of the subject: an alphabetical list of the Roman churches discussed together with the names of other churches notable for their use of recycled materials; a timeline showing key dates relating to historic events and individuals interwoven with the founding dates of the eleven featured churches; a list of the popes mentioned in the book; a glossary of architectural terms; an illustrated guide to the most commonly used types of stone; a bibliography; an index of names and topics covered; and, on the front and back inside covers, a map of the city showing the locations of the featured churches.

Many of the churches lie outside the ancient walls of the city, which means that to get to them you will have to walk some distance, take a bus or taxi or – most definitely to be recommended – cycle. And in the heat of summer, to be sure of getting into the churches it is a good idea to take the trouble to drape a sweater over bare shoulders and wear trousers rather than shorts, out of respect for the morals and mores of the Catholic Church. On the other hand, visitors are not only in for a very special architectonic and historic treat, they also have the chance to experience the cool, concentrated peace which is the mark of these age-old sacred spaces: an atmosphere which contrasts sharply with the restlessness of modern city life. That alone is worth any small effort involved.

Historical background

I T WAS with the Emperor Constantine (reigned AD 306–337) that the new practice of manifest recycling was introduced into Late Antiquity building. Constantine was also the man behind another breakthrough. Although baptized only on his deathbed he is regarded as the first Christian emperor, because he legalized Christianity (AD 313) and instigated the building of the first public churches, in Rome and elsewhere in the Roman Empire. There had been tendencies towards the use of spolia under his predecessors, but during Constantine's reign the recycling of ancient architectural elements and reliefs was taken to another level, both qualitatively and quantitatively. In the very first church he founded (c. AD 313), the great Lateran Basilica – San Giovanni in Laterano, Rome's cathedral – a wide variety of columns and *capitals* were used, these being either spolia or material from the city's stock of prefabricated building elements [4] [5]. At the same time as the Lateran Basilica was being built Constantine was also overseeing the erection of his triumphal arch (AD 315), in which, for the first time, spolia reliefs were deliberately combined with newly produced material to form a carefully devized design [6]. The Arch of Constantine is almost completely covered in these reliefs. The top half of the arch bears reliefs from the times of the Emperors Trajan, Hadrian and Marcus Aurelius, all three of them emperors from the third century and considered by later generations to be particularly worthy of emulation. Constantine even had the imperial portraits in the reliefs recarved to resemble himself – thereby clothing himself, so to speak in the grand Roman tradition and at the same time showing that, while he might hail from the East and be of humble origins, he could be likened to an ancient Roman ideal. The reliefs on the lower half of the arch were new works created by Constantine's own sculptors; the same applies to the frieze which runs all the way round the arch, forming the basis for the upper spolia reliefs. Thus Constantine also managed to make the point that his rule did not merely repeat the past, it stood for renewal too.

4 Filippo Gagliardi: *San Giovanni in Laterano*. Fresco painted on the wall of the church of San Martino ai Monti at the time of Borromini's rebuilding of **7** the Lateran Basilica (c. 1650). This fresco gives some idea of how the Early Christian church (c. 313) would have looked, although it was constructed with entablatures running across the columns in the nave. The arcades depicted in Gagliardi's fresco date from a later medieval modernization.

This synthesis between the old and the new is central to the design of the Arch of Constantine and its use of spolia and this same principle seems to have been a key factor in the recycling of antique elements in the centuries to come. The use of second-hand building materials is, in fact, not in itself unique to the Middle Ages. It is probably safe to say that recycling has always been practiced, wherever there have been some good stones or beams lying handy [**7**]. What is special about the architecture of Medieval Rome is that no attempt was made to camouflage or conceal this recycling. The spolia churches are, moreover, remarkable for the way in which old elements were reused in new contexts or new ways. We are looking here at a juxtaposition of contrasting architectural elements and principles the like of which would not be seen again until our own time, where it manifests itself, for example, in the current trend for putting old industrial buildings to new uses – turning them into arts centres, flats and so on – or in so-called deconstructivist

5 🟦7 San Giovanni in Laterano (the Lateran Basilica): the green marble columns (*verde antico*) from the Constantinian basilica (c. 313) were reused in the sculpture niches when the church was rebuilt by Borromini around 1650 and given its present form.

VOTIS·XX

6 The Arch of Constantine (315). The upper part of the arch is adorned with spolia reliefs from the time of the Emperor Hadrian and Marcus Aurelius (second century). On the inner side of the central arch are reliefs from the time of the Emperor Trajan (second century) which were recarved to portray Constantine himself. Running all the way round the arch under the roundels is a frieze executed by the Constantinian sculptors. The figures in relief below this also date from the time of the arch's construction.

Another notable feature of the arch, apart from the different historical origins of its various elements, is the variation in the colour of the stones: the columns, for example, are of yellow marble (*giallo antico*), the roundels are framed by a border of red *porphyry* (only partly preserved); the frieze above these was possibly faced with green porphyry and the sculptures at the top of captured Dacians are of purple-veined white marble (*pavonazzetto*) and are set on green-streaked plinths (*cipollino*).

7 The Aurelian wall around Rome (271–275 with later additions), by the Porta Ardeatina. The different stages in the wall's building and repairs to the wall are clearly discernible. In the close-up below (in the wall near the Porta Latina) one can see how marble fragments complete with the vestiges of carved decorations have been built into the wall along with all manner of other material.

architecture, where classic, symmetrical uniformity is resolutely shunned in favour of distorted, unpredictable, incongruously complex constructions.

All of Constantine's machinations on the cultural politics front did not, however, win him the favour of the old, hidebound Roman aristocracy and in the mid-320s AD he decided quite simply to relocate the imperial capital to the newly founded Constantinople (now Istanbul) which lay in a more propitious corner of the Roman Empire, in military as well as political and economic terms. Here the Roman Empire continued to exist for centuries as the Byzantine or Eastern Empire, while the empire in the West gradually disintegrated over the course of the fifth century. The last Western Roman emperor was Romulus Augustulus (reigned 475–476). And although the Byzantine emperor continued to have the ultimate authority over Rome, in the real world of politics the Roman Pope was to a greater and greater extent becoming the true power in the city – as well as the unifying father figure of the Medieval Church in Western Europe. And indeed, by the end of the eighth century the papacy had, to all intents and purposes, taken control in Rome, at the cost of the Byzantine emperor's authority.

These power struggles had a direct bearing on Roman church buildings. Not just anybody was allowed to demolish ancient architecture, not even those with the laudable aim of using the materials to erect churches. During the first centuries of the *Early Christian* and early Medieval periods only the emperor had the right to dispose of the old and by then possibly dilapidated public buildings from the great days of the Empire. As late as the 660s, during a visit to Rome, the Byzantine Emperor Constans II saw fit to swipe the gilded copper tiles off the roof of the Pantheon and carry them back with him to Constantinople. As time went on, though, the appropriation of ancient Roman buildings became a privilege granted to the papacy.

In Late Antiquity, as the Roman Empire was on the decline economically and politically, population levels in the city also fell drastically. Where in its heyday Rome is estimated to have had about a million inhabitants, during the Middle Ages this figure is believed to have dwindled to no more than thirty thousand or so. This meant, of course, that a lot of buildings stood empty and unused. Many of the ancient public buildings no longer had any function in the Christian society and there were neither people enough to put the buildings to new uses nor hands enough and funds enough

8 The Temple of Saturn (probably c. 360–380), Forum Romanum. The column shafts are spolia of noticeably differing heights and widths and of both red and grey granite. The entablature too is a recycled piece and here the ornamented side, which originally faced outwards, has been turned inwards, so that the smooth outer side could be carved with an inscription. The Ionic *capitals* are from the time of the temple's construction and have been cut to fit the diameter of each column.

to maintain them. Nonetheless, they did try, as far as possible, to preserve some appearance of their bygone power and prosperity, until the sixth century at any rate. There were strict laws against defacing public buildings and a ban on building anything new if there was an old property in need of renovation. For a while longer attempts were even made to preserve the temples, which had lost their function as far back as the fourth century when pagan rites were forbidden by law.

All in all, there was a great respect for all things ancient which, in an ancestor worshipping society such as the Roman one, is not really so surprising. There was a distinct awareness of the link between the standing of the city and the number and quality of its monumental public buildings. Hence the reason that even buildings such as temples, which the Christians associated with extremely dangerous demonic forces, were appreciated as being a positive aspect of the city's profile – so long, that is, as they were not used for their old, problematic purpose.

That laws governing the preservation of ancient buildings and prohibiting spoiling were passed again and again during the fourth and fifth centuries can, however, only be interpreted as a sign that there was a problem: if the authorities had been respected and the buildings left undisturbed the constant re-decreeing of these laws would not have been necessary. And yet there is nothing to suggest that during these first centuries of Christianity ancient buildings such as temples were actually torn down in order to provide the materials necessary to build churches. Those spolia which were in fact used must have come from buildings already in disrepair, where any attempts at maintenance had been abandoned. It is worth noting that even the last few temples to be erected during the second half of the fourth century – in a final burst of resistance from the old, pagan Roman Senate aristocracy against the new times, the new Establishment and its faith – were constructed out of spolia and diverse materials from the city's stores of marble.

In these times of crisis the production of new building materials in the Western Roman Empire simply ground to a halt. Stone was still being cut, however, in the Byzantine Empire, so for a while longer it was possible to import serially-produced, standard pieces from there. Throughout the fifth century there were, therefore instances – for example in Santa Maria Maggiore [16] and in Santo Stefano Rotondo ⑪ [103] of serially produced materials of Byzantine (Greek) origin being used, mainly items already in stock. But

9 Well-head in ❷ San Bartolomeo all'Isola (c. 1000). Marble. The images of the saints are framed by columns of two different types: on the right a spiral column and on the left a shaft featuring a combination of leaf ornamentation on the bottom half and spiral fluting above. The artist has deliberately chosen to carve different types of column rather than repeat the same style. Apparently variation was a desirable quality and not a solution used for want of anything better.

Historical background

10 🔞 Santa Maria in Aracoeli (c. 1260–1270). In its essentials and in its use and arrangement of ancient spolia, this church – which contains many new additions from the Renaissance and later, including altars, chapel decorations and the magnificent wooden ceiling – dates from the time known in Northern Europe as the Gothic era. In Rome, however, church builders still kept their ancient past alive, both through the use of spolia

and through the employment of round arches in their arcades instead of the pointed arches of the 'modern' Gothic architecture common in Northern Europe. The wide disparity in the heights of the shafts was evened out by the use of bases and *plinths* of different sizes and shapes or by combining them with low Ionic or higher Corinthian or Composite. The shafts are of red and grey granite and smooth or fluted marble.

in the slightly longer term only old, antique elements were used in the Medieval Roman churches. Not until the twelfth century do we again see examples of churches containing a large proportion of newly produced material, such as series of Ionic capitals.

There can be little doubt that the use of spolia came as a consequence of the economic slump in Late Antiquity and the shortfall in manufacturing and productivity occasioned by this depression and the drop in population. Interestingly enough, though, if one takes a closer look at the spolia architecture which resulted from these social conditions one finds that the artistic possibilities thus presented were actually very closely bound up with a new aesthetic. People understood how to exploit the given circumstances in such a way that from them sprang beautiful and significant buildings. When we, in our own time, in the affluent developed world, feel that the recycling of everything from buildings to clothes is preferable to buying newly manufactured products – and, indeed, consider the old cobbled together articles more beautiful and more meaningful or satisfying to use or to live in than something brand-new – then it's easy for us to see how people of an earlier age could have felt the same. But this sympathy for recycling and the attendant appreciation of the incongruous buildings of the early Middle Ages is a relatively new phenomenon. There has been a tendency in the writing of history to dismiss the rich variety of spolia architecture as a stop-gap solution. This book takes issue with that view. Instead it is proposed here that in the Early Christian period and in the early Middle Ages, people made a virtue of necessity: a closer look at the way in which the spolia have been used reveals that back then it was not merely a matter of settling for, but of actually preferring diversity to uniformity, because the variations in material, colour, and finish produced a particularly attractive architectonic and spatial effect and evinced a complex and pleasing temporality.

Similarly, if you look for depictions of columns in art (frescoes, illuminated manuscripts, reliefs) where the artists have been more or less free to depict architecture exactly as they pleased, you will find that variation is a recurring theme. And when, in such works, where they could easily just have painted or carved homogenous forms, the artists have opted instead for diversity, it seems clear that multiformity was highly prized [9].

We cannot expect to find any written accounts from the Middle Ages which provide explicit explanations of the motives behind the use of spolia. Such meditations on architectural theory were simply unknown in those days and architectural criticism did not exist until modern times. The Chronicle of the Popes, *Liber Pontificalis*, an important source on ecclesiastical architecture begun in the sixth century, is a good example of contemporary writing on this subject. It contains a record of papal building activities, but it provides no explanation for why the buildings took the form that they did. On the other hand, lots of other sources of different kinds have survived – writings on theology, rhetoric, music, literature and much else – from which it is quite apparent that in those days people had a fondness for eclectic compositions; that they attached great importance to the marrying of old and new and that they felt this was the 'right' approach to take if one wished to achieve an ethically and aesthetically pleasing result. As we shall see in the following chapters, the systematic (but definitely not standardized) way in which spolia were used in the churches underscores just how laden with significance this recycling and this rich diversity could be.

The use of antique spolia in Medieval buildings is not an exclusively Roman phenomenon; it occurred throughout the area originally covered by the Roman Empire. North of the Alps they stopped using spolia during the Romanesque era and, more especially, the Gothic period (from c. 1100 onwards), when a new view of architecture and better economic conditions went hand in hand with a desire for serially produced, standardized architectural elements. In Roman ecclesiastical architecture, however, incongruous combinations of architectural elements still had a place until as late as the thirteenth century [10]. Even in the High Renaissance designs by Bramante for a new St Peter's (around 1500) it appears that the possibility of reusing spolia columns from the old fourth-century basilica to adorn the exterior of the new church's massive dome was considered [11]. This scheme came to nothing however. And if spolia were actually used in late-Gothic and Renaissance (fourteenth and fifteenth centuries) architecture in Rome it was in such a modified, touchedup form that they did not look like recycled pieces. And with that, the most important chapter in the history of architectural spolia comes to a close, because if one can no longer *see* that ancient elements have been used, then a great deal of the aesthetic value of recycling, not to mention the significance attached to building on the past is, of course, lost.

Use of spolia in the Early Christian basilica

THE FOUNDING by the Emperor Constantine of the great Lateran Basilica (San Giovanni in Laterano) ushered in an entirely new style of building: the public church. Until the legalization of Christianity in AD 313 early Christians held their services in private homes. Such houses, *domus ecclesiae*, would usually contain a large room in which the congregation could meet, but apart from that, in architectural terms, there was nothing particularly remarkable about them. On the contrary, during times of Christian persecution, the more nondescript they were the better.

In the fourth century when the building of churches began, this new style of building was not modelled on the ancient pagan temple. For one thing, the early Christians probably felt the need to dissociate themselves from the old cult, and for another the classic form of temple was not really suitable for large gatherings. In the traditional temple all the decoration tends to be concentrated on the outside, which is normally adorned with columns and dressed with marble, just as rites were conducted outside, in front of the temple. The temple did have a central chamber, the *cella*, but this was relatively small and dark, with no windows, and only the priests could enter it.

Instead the new churches, where the focus was on the interior – on the gathering of the congregation for services – took their outset in the Roman *basilica* which was, from a practical point of view, well-suited for use as a meeting-house. Originally, a basilica was a kind of large covered hall, lined with colonnades and serving many different – and initially secular – functions: markets were held there, for example, and courts of law. But by late antiquity the emperor was increasingly being accorded the status of a god and when used for imperial functions the basilica could take on an almost sacred character. And it was in this guise – but with Christ taking the place of the emperor – that the basilica was adopted and adapted to Christian use.

The standard Christian basilica is a longitudinal church with a central nave, often flanked by one or – in very large churches – two side aisles. Colonnades separate the nave from the side-aisles [**11**]. The nave itself runs from the entrance up to the church's most sacred area: the chancel, with the altar and the *apse*, a semi-circular, vaulted space. Set into the walls (the *clerestory*) above the colonnades in the nave are windows which in Early Christian churches (unlike later medieval churches) are of a substantial size and let plenty of light into the church **10** [**99**].

The Lateran Basilica was the first, but not the only large imperial church of this period [**4**]. The fourth century and early fifth century saw the building of such great basilicas as St Peter's [**11**], San Paolo fuori le Mura [**13**] and Santa Maria Maggiore [**16**]. These churches are still key destinations for many pilgrims wishing to honour the apostles Peter and Paul and commemorate their martyrdom in Rome. But another of the most important churches

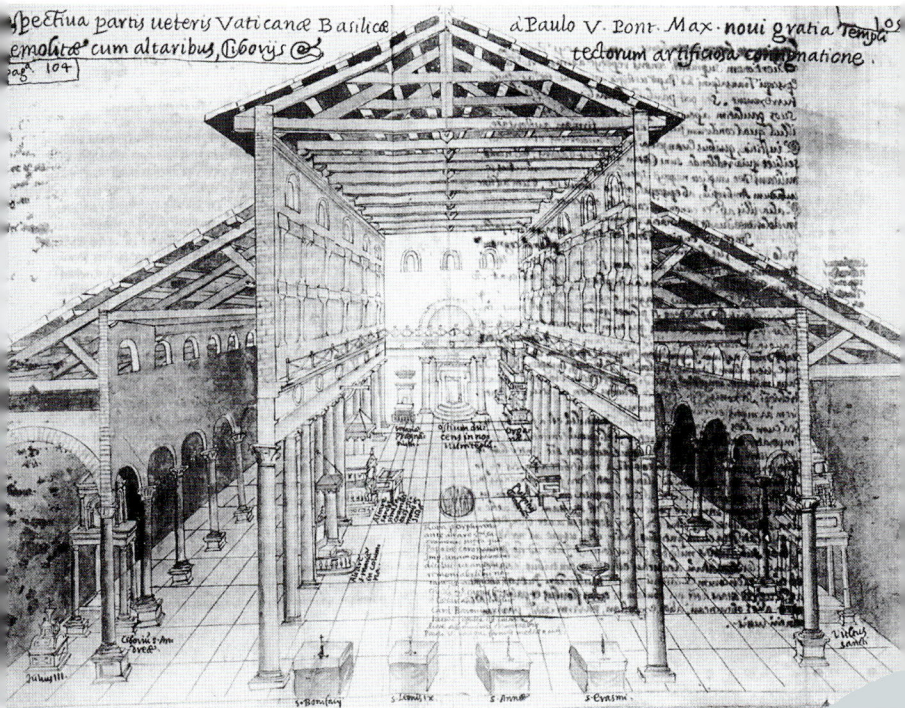

11 The Early Christian church of St Peter's **21** in a drawing by Giacomo Grimaldi from 1620, around the time when the old nave was torn down to make way for the building of the new St Peter's. The columns in the church were of many different stones and styles. While the side-aisles were furnished with columned arcades, the columns in the nave supported a traditional entablature.

for Christian visitors is the slightly smaller, but beautiful and – in terms of spolia – extremely interesting San Lorenzo fuori le Mura **❻**. The foundation of both San Paolo and San Lorenzo can be traced back to the Emperor Constantine, although his original buildings were later replaced by others. Recent research suggests that St Peter's, which is also credited to Constantine (c. 320–333), may instead date from 337–350, which is to say: from the reign of his successor and son Constans (in the West, Constantius II in the Byzantine Empire). This is a highly controversial assertion and one that is still a long way from winning official credence: it has, of course, been of tremendous importance to the Church that the apostolic seat should be seen as having been founded by the first Christian emperor.

But when and to what extent were spolia used in the first churches? Was it a case of an economic stop-gap solution or a definitive move towards a new style? And when spolia were used, did the materials vary or did the builders initially opt for a more classical, uniform appearance?

In fact, even the very first great imperial churches, the Lateran Basilica (c. AD 313) and St Peter's (whether it dates from around AD 320–330 or the mid-fourth century) were built from spolia or possibly stock pieces, i.e. elements not specially produced for the building concerned. This was a radical new departure. The older Roman basilicas, to which the churches can be compared architecturally, contained rows of identical, newly manufactured columns.

Both the Lateran Basilica and St Peter's were rebuilt during the Baroque period, so what knowledge we have of their Early Christian appearance is purely second-hand. But in both cases it looks as though a variety of materials was employed. As emperor, Constantine invested an enormous amount in new buildings throughout the Roman Empire. It's interesting to note, therefore, that the builders chose to make use of a wide range of different architectural elements and spolia rather than homogeneous, freshly produced materials for such large and important churches. Prior to this, it had been customary with buildings on the scale of the Lateran Basilica to set up a stonemason's workshop on site, for the preparation of the necessary raw materials, which were imported in their rough-hewn state – from the Eastern Roman (Greek or Byzantine) area, for example. From the use of spolia here and in later imperial

churches in the fourth and fifth centuries, when newly manufactured materials were still available, it is quite evident that this
practice of recycling was regarded as the most attractive, exclusive
and up-to-date method of building at that time. In Constantine's
day the emperor still had the resources at his disposal for large-scale
building projects; he could have insisted on using new and homogeneous elements had he so wished.

We can gain some impression of the original Lateran Basilica
from a – not entirely reliable – reproduction in a fresco from the
seventeenth century [4]. This painting dates from the time when
the old church was radically modernized, with the great architect
Francesco Borromini 'encapsulating' and concealing the Early
Christian basilica within a new, stylistically coherent Baroque shell.
The fresco shows the church with columned arcades running down
either side of the nave. This arrangement dated from renovations
carried out during the High Middle Ages, when the arcades
replaced the traditional combination of columns topped by *entablatures*, which we know the Constantinian church contained. The
depiction of the arcades in the side aisles is reasonably faithful. We
can therefore deduce that the Constantinian church was one of the
very first buildings to employ this combination of arcades supported by columns, one which would by medieval times have become
the standard solution. Although the conventional ancient Roman
form of columns supporting entablatures was used in the nave of
the church, the side aisles represented yet another aspect of the stylistic innovation, one which also included the unclassical diversity
of materials and the use of spolia. Colour was another feature of the
interior, with variation here too: in the green marble column shafts
in the side aisles and the red *granite* shafts of some, at least, of the
columns flanking the nave. In fact, in Borromini's modernized
basilica the green columns from the side-aisles of the Early Christian church were reused to frame the niches containing the monumental sculptures of the apostles [5]. The columns were restored,
so they look like new, but they are nonetheless 'relics' from the original building. Whether the capitals were also as diverse in form as
the seventeenth-century fresco implies is not, however, known.

In the case of St Peter's, here too the nave was flanked by a traditional combination of columns and entablatures, while the two side
aisles were bounded by the new-fashioned columned arcades [11].
Here we know that the entablatures in the nave constituted a veri-

table patchwork of spolia or stock pieces and that the column shafts, in highly unclassical fashion, varied greatly in finish and fabric, consisting both of different types of pale grey marble and some very colourful sorts such as *africano*. The capitals in the nave were equally varied, probably a mix of *Corinthian* and *Composite* in different sizes depending on the height of the individual shafts. But the arrangement of the columns was governed by one guiding rule, as we can see from a whole succession of later spolia churches: the different types of stone were arranged symmetrically in pairs running down either side of the central aisle of the church ❷ [**47**]. So, rather than deploying the materials in such a way as to create a more coherent run of elements within each colonnade, the builders preferred to forge a link between the two sides of the nave. And in so doing they also achieved a rhythmic progression down the length of the church.

This marked a crucial new departure in the Christian basilica: where the traditional, secular basilica could just as easily have been constructed with an entrance either on a side wall or an end wall, and the colonnades always consisted of identical columns, the longitudinal and hierarchical progression up the church from the entrance to the holy of holies, the altar and the apse, is a key feature of the Christian basilica. This ties in with the fundamental Christian concept of life as a steady progression towards salvation and the idea that a process of change takes place from the moment one steps inside the church until one reaches its most sacred spot. This process could be accentuated visually by the variation of and progressive shift in the recycled elements. It is easy to see why a mixture of different materials could seem more attractive and meaningful in the Christian basilica than it would have been in a traditional Roman building. In the latter, more store was set by qualities such as stability, timelessness and logical, predictable sequences, all of which uniformity of material was seen to represent.

Principles for the distribution of spolia

I N ORDER TO UNDERSTAND just how radically innovative the new Christian and medieval spolia architecture actually was, we need to look for a moment at the attitude of the day to the classical *architectural orders* of columns and *capitals*, which is to say: the structured system of vertical, load-bearing architectural elements and the horizontal elements which these support, their proportions and their ornamentation. This system was established in Greece, where it is most commonly known from the temples (it was only later, however, around 1500, that the term *column orders* was coined). Each order consisted of a column shaft which rested on a base and was topped by a capital. This last could either be *Doric*: simple, round, cushion-shaped; *Ionic*: voluted, with an 'egg and dart' frieze (an ornamental border of alternating oval and triangular reliefs); or *Corinthian*: "overgrown" with *acanthus* leaves. The design of the capital depended on the particular set of proportions and ornamentation – i.e. the column order – concerned. And finally, on top of the capital rested the trabeation or *entablature*, consisting of architrave, frieze and cornice [**12**].

The Romans adopted this system. But to the Greeks' Doric, Ionic and Corinthian orders they added their own eclectic order, namely the *Composite* style which, in a typical example of Roman cultural fusion and artistic appropriation, combines the acanthus leaves of the Corinthian capital with the volutes (or scrolls) and egg-and-dart frieze of the Ionic. This new and uniquely Roman column order, with its composite style of capital was, not suprisingly, used in triumphal arches (all except the Arch of Constantine), evidently as a reminder of the assumption, usurpation and transformation of other civilizations that went hand in hand with Rome's cultural and military triumphs.

It is important to note here that the rules governing the column orders were not confined to the design of the capitals; each detail conformed to a system of measurements. Capitals and columns were precisely proportioned and teamed with specified bases and entablatures, which were in turn sub-divided into proportionally defined mouldings and friezes. In the classical Greek and Roman system identical capital styles and corresponding shafts were used for every column in a colonnade. Only sporadically, from around AD 300 did combinations of shafts and capitals of different types, ornamentation, colour or finish start to appear – and not to any great extent until the advent of the new spolia churches ❺ [67], ❼ [82].

Not that there was any shortage of structural variety or stylistic invention in earlier Roman architecture, from before AD 300. The churches of the Middle Ages would not have had such a motley appearance if the ancient buildings from which the materials for their construction were taken had not been full of colour and abounding in different styles. But the variation in materials and styles within the *same* series of columns found in the Early Christian and medieval churches represents a break with classical, predictable uniformity and its rootedness in certain set rules of proportion. Rules which took their outset in the admiration of the human body; the capital, for example, was seen as the column's head (hence the name, which comes from the Latin *caput* meaning head). The Early Christian and medieval practice whereby shafts are combined with capitals and bases which did not originally go together and which do not therefore correspond in terms of proportion, size or material, also constitutes a breach of the original system's ideals of balance and harmony.

Another crucial departure from the classical tradition was seen in the separation of column and capital from the entablature that occurred when the columns were instead employed to support arcades [11]. This new structural innovation, the columned arcade, began to make its presence felt from around AD 300 onwards. There are only a few, rare earlier instances of this mode of construction from before the days of spolia architecture. Not that arcades were anything new in themselves. Prior to this, the Romans had made wide use of the round arch in their architecture. But in the traditional (ancient Roman) use of the arcade it was underpinned by square piers, so that the arcade was simply the rounded culmination of an opening in the wall ❿ [101]. If, however, a circular column and its capital are employed to support such an arcade, a

12 *The column orders.* Left to right: Doric, Ionic, Corinthian and Composite. Detail from an illustration in *Ordonnance des cinq especes de colonnes selon la methode des anciens* by Claude Perrault (1683), Plate 1. Perrault also described a fifth order, the Tuscan: a simplified version of the Doric not included here.

A B C D E

Modules

6 Modules

6 Modules

6 Modules

6 Modules

20 Minutes

8 diametre

8 Diametre   40 Minutes

9 Diametre

10 Diametre

24 Modules

26 Modules

28 Modules

30 Modules

7 Modules

8 Modules

9 Modules

10 Modules

45

40

35

30

25

20

15

10

5

discreet break is created in the connection between the capital and the arcade's square base. The original, predictably proportional link between column, capital and entablature is also eliminated. There is no obvious proportional relationship between the column, the capital and the high wall pierced with windows, the *clerestory*, which they support.

All in all, we can say therefore that in the architecture of late antiquity the individual elements underwent a process of separation and liberation. The logical, predictable and 'rational' order (note that the word *ratio* refers both to proportions and to the faculty of reason/common sense) of earlier Roman architecture fitted perfectly with a rational view of the world rooted in the harmony and balance of the human figure. In the new Christian world view, on the other hand, these values and attributes were replaced by a fascination with the unpredictable, irrational and incomprehensible and a gradual rejection of the secular, corporeal, material aspects which had played such an important part in the old Roman society.

An arcade supported by columns consisting of diverse spolia can not, therefore, be explained simply by a lack of financial or technical wherewithal for the production of new architectural elements. It can also be perceived as a metaphor for certain new Christian values and a new world view. The financial and technical possibilities of that particular time were closely bound up with the aesthetic and ideological needs of the day. They could not build the way the ancient Romans had done but nor, it appears, did they have any wish to.

In fact the Early Christian and medieval churches could convey many messages through the diversity and the recycled aspect of spolia. As mentioned in the previous chapter a progressive shift in style and/or material along the nave could seem attractive as a metaphor for the progress towards salvation which Christians make on their way from the entrance to the altar. The hierarchy of materials that is detectable in a church such as Sant'Agnese illustrates this point **2** [**47**]. But spolia could also be used to create spatial effects that accorded with or underscored the *liturgy*. In the Lateran Baptistery the variation in the column capitals appears to correspond to the ritual of baptism **1** [**39**] [**40**]: stepping down into the central baptismal basin one passed between the two simpler Ionic columns and, on stepping up afterwards, newly baptized, passed between the two Composite columns. The Composite order was apparently still associated with triumph (as we saw in its employment in

Roman triumphal arches), but now in an ecclesiastical context, representing Christian victory over death through baptism.

The practice of arranging materials in pairs across the axis of the church was also significant since this meant that one was framed or embraced by the matching pairs of columns as one moved up the nave ❷ [47]. In some of the later churches there is, however, a clear difference in the materials on the right and left sides. One possible explanation for such a layout could be that in these cases the spolia were meant to denote the different status and 'gender' of the two sides. The right side, which was traditionally regarded throughout the Middle Ages as being positively charged, was reserved for the men, while the negatively charged left side was designated the women's area. This distinct difference between the two sides can be seen in San Giorgio in Velabro (c. 827–844) ❺ [67] and San Nicola in Carcere (late eleventh century) ❾ [92]. In both cases we find a uniform use of materials on the left-hand side, while the right-hand side features a wider, 'richer' variety of materials. The common association of the right side with positive qualities is a clear indication that a diversity of materials was considered desirable and viewed as an asset while a uniform appearance was connected with lower status and, by extension, the female sex.

Another liturgical point seems to have been made in churches where there was a clear demarcation between the front area of the nave and the rear. This sort of division accords with a practice which was probably making itself felt in a church such as Sant'Agnese from as early as the seventh century, but was certainly common in the late Middle Ages: namely that of laymen being placed closest to the entrance while the area around the altar was reserved for the clergy. In Sant' Agnese the last two pairs of columns are of the finest red marble ❷ [49]. A slightly earlier description (Choricius, c. 540) of a church from the Eastern Roman Empire, St Stefan in Gaza, also speaks of a colonnade following this pattern:

> Of the columns the most notable are the four coloured by nature with the hues of the imperial robes [i.e. purply/porphyry] which define the bounds of that area that is forbidden to those who are not of the clergy.

The similarity between this description of the church in Gaza and the positioning of the four red marble columns in Sant'Agnese is striking. Although in the latter the red columns are not of *porphyry*, their colour was obviously associated with the dignity and divinity

Principles for the distribution of spolia

13 On display at **20** San Paolo fuori le Mura, in the so-called 'Passegiata archeologica', are those fragments of columns, bases and capitals which were salvaged from the Early Christian Basilica when it burned down in 1823. From these one can gain some idea of the wide range of materials used for column shafts and capitals, many of which were produced specially for the massive, five-naved basilica (380s). Spolia were also included in the church, however, if not during its construction then during the repair work undertaken after the building was struck by lightning about fifty years after its completion, during the reign of Pope Leo the Great (440–461).

usually attributed to the purple of porphyry. It was a colour – and porphyry was a stone – which in late antiquity was reserved for the emperor, but which in Early Christian times was adopted for depictions of Christ and sacred figures in general (see p. 60). This is also why, in the mosaic on the side wall of the apse, St Agnes and the two popes are shown clad in purple robes ❷ [47]. The description of the church in Gaza thus helps to confirm the supposition that the variety of spolia and their arrangement were by no means random. There are many other examples of similar arrangements which seem to create separate sections for clergy and laymen.

One such example can be seen in San Lorenzo fuori le Mura. This sixth-century basilica was extended in the thirteenth century, with the addition of the so-called Honorius Basilica ❻ [75]. Here, in the nave the two columns bounding the last third of the church differ in diameter and height from all the other columns. A change in the flooring reveals that this distinctive pair of short, slender columns mark the spot where a special enclosure (in later terminology known as the *schola cantorum*) separated the clergy from the rest of the congregation [76].

San Paolo fuori le Mura represents a unique chapter in the history of spolia use and the aesthetic of diversity. In this imperial building (founded by the emperors Valentinian II, Theodosius and Honorius in the mid-380s) for the last time for centuries to come a special workshop was set up on-site for the production or fashioning of the necessary architectural elements of *Proconnesian* marble

14 ⓴ San Paolo fuori le Mura. The Ionic capital in the centre is one of a pair which were set on spolia shafts and bases on either side of the church's *triumphal arch* during renovations to the church in the mid-fifth century.

imported from the Eastern Roman Empire. This vast church burned down in 1823 and was then rebuilt in the scrupulously uniform, historicist classicism of the period. Interestingly, though, fragments saved from the Early Christian building show, that it contained pieces in various styles, even though these were new elements produced specially for this building [13] [14]: within the same colonnade one found both Corinthian and Composite capitals, and while the capitals in the nave were of the normal style with *fluted* shafts, those in the side aisles had full-leaf capitals on smooth shafts. By this time the desire for variation was taken so much for granted that a wealth of different styles was actually incorporated into the designs for the building, despite the decision to use newly produced pieces rather than spolia. The builders manufactured a 'spolia effect', so to speak. They also opted for the innovative combination of columns and arcades in all four colonnades in the five-aisled church, while the Lateran Basilica (c. 313) and St Peter's (c. 340s?) could as yet only boast this arrangement in their side aisles, the columns in the nave still carrying the traditional entablatures [11].

Although there was a general tendency throughout the early Middle Ages towards a greater and greater variety of architectural elements, some early churches were already notable for their exceptional diversity of materials. One of these is the Early Christian church of San Clemente (from around AD 400) which was built at the same time as San Paolo, but on a very different, more modest scale than the imperial churches ❸ [56]. In the early twelfth century a new church (the present San Clemente) was built on top of the old basilica. But from the remains of the first church – the cellar-like chambers now accessible from the 'new' church – one can still gain some impression of how widely the columns here varied in terms of their fabric and the style and decoration of the individual elements [57] [58]. Apart from the diversity of materials, finishes and capital styles it displays, which is unusually wide for a church built around 400, San Clemente is also unique in that columns in different sorts of marble appear to some extent to have been arranged in pairs within the same colonnade (rather than facing one another across the central axis as was usually the case). Such a motley assortment of elements and forms would not be seen again for several hundred years ❼ [80], ❾ [92].

Unlike the above-mentioned churches with their pronounced mix of materials there were a number of other Early Christian churches which featured a more uniform use of spolia. This phen-

15 🌐 San Pietro in Vincoli (432–440). This church, founded with imperial support during the pontificate of Sixtus III, is notable for its extraordinarily homogeneous collection of spolia: in all, twenty identical *fluted* marble columns, crowned with Doric capitals. These columns may have come from a nearby building such as the *Portico di Livia*. The *triumphal*

arch is supported by grey granite shafts with Corinthian capitals. The church, famed for Michelangelo's Tomb of Pope Julius II with its magnificent sculpture of Moses (c. 1514), was modernized in the sixteenth century and the early eighteenth century, when a barrel-vaulted ceiling was constructed and the apse decorated with frescoes.

16 Santa Maria Maggiore, with twenty shafts of pale-grey marble and Ionic capitals restored to their present uniform appearance by Ferdinando Fuga (1747–1750).

omenon is, however, more the exception than the rule. The most striking examples of this are Santa Sabina (c. AD 422–432) **10** [99] and San Pietro in Vincoli (AD 432–440) [15], the homogeneous appearance of both stemming from the fact that each contains two complete sets of identical columns with matching capitals and bases. And, quite uniquely, in the case of San Pietro in Vincoli these happen to be Doric columns (first century). The Doric order had become more or less obsolete by the time of the Roman Empire; in Christian spolia architecture the use of Doric capitals is practically non-existent. It may not be entirely coincidental, though, that this rare style of column should have be found here of all places. San Pietro in Vincoli was dedicated, after all, to St Peter and the masculine attributes traditionally associated with the Doric order could be considered an apt metaphor for this powerful apostle, described (in the New Testament) as 'the rock' (in Greek 'petros'), on which the Church was built. The chains with which on two occasions he was shackled, but from which he broke free and which are displayed as holy relics in San Pietro, are also a reminder of his remarkable strength.

But even in their employment of these identical sets of columns, Santa Sabina and San Pietro in Vincoli both deviate from the classical tradition in that their builders decided against using the entablatures which these columns must originally have carried. Considering the excellent condition of the stone these columns would in all likelihood have been in a good enough state to be reused if so desired. And yet the decision was made to combine the old elements with the arcade construction, thus producing a totally new and different effect. Not only that, but in San Pietro in Vincoli the uniformity of a set of twenty Doric columns is offset by a distinct variation in materials and styles in the columns supporting the *triumphal arch*. Here, a pair of grey granite shafts carry Eastern Roman (Greek/Byzantine) Corinthian capitals from around the same time – a significant culmination of the nave in simple, modest granite shafts and 'Christian' capitals.

Again in Santa Maria Maggiore – built, like the Lateran Baptistery ❶, during the reign of Pope Sixtus III (AD 432–440) – all the columns in the nave are of the same order [16]. Here the capitals are Ionic and in traditional Roman style these are even topped by an entablature. The uniform appearance of the church today can however be attributed to the fact that the columns were totally refurbished in what may have been the most spolia hostile period in art history: the late Baroque (c. 1750, by Ferdinando Fuga). Today the shafts are all of the same polished, pale-grey Proconnesian marble, but the original colonnades featured a combination of these and six shafts of grey-green *cipollino* marble. The original late-Antique Ionic capitals (imported serially-produced pieces or stock items)

17 Santa Maria Maggiore. Detail of restoration work on a shaft placed on one of the new, eighteenth-century bases.

18 **14** Santa Maria in Domnica,
looking towards the fine mosaic from
the time of Pope Paschal I (817–824).
Nine columns line each side of the
nave, all with relatively similar granite
shafts and all with Corinthian capitals,
though from various periods. A couple
of splendid *porphyry* columns support
the *triumphal arch*.

were evidently too rough or too variable in character to pass muster for an eighteenth-century modernization. And so they were replaced, along with the wide assortment of bases, by the present versions [17].

That one of the earliest churches of all should have been dedicated to a woman, the Virgin Mary (who was not defined as the Mother of God until AD 430 at the Council of Ephesus), might go some way to explaining its subdued, homogeneous appearance. Just as the Ionic order was most often employed during this period in less prominent parts of a church or outside the church itself, so the choice of this order for Santa Maria Maggiore could be interpreted as being suitably discreet. Since variety in the use of spolia appears, generally speaking, to have been considered a good thing, the relative uniformity of style here seems an appropriate way of denoting the 'feminine modesty' of this church, as opposed to the more imposing St Peter's, the Lateran Basilica (originally dedicated to the Saviour himself) or Santa Maria Maggiore's immediate predecessor, built to the glory of the apostle Paul: San Paolo fuori le Mura.

A couple of ninth-century Roman churches also display a tendency towards the use of homogeneous architectural elements, the lovely Santa Maria in Domnica (817–824), for example. This ninth-century homogeneity has been viewed by some as a sign of a certain 'classicism' at that time, a conscious ecclesiastical attempt to gain legitimacy and authority through such references to antiquity (which is to say through the uniformity of materials associated with Ancient Rome). This theory is a controversial one, however, and not all Roman churches from that period are as uniform in appearance.

Another tendency towards homogeneity in the medieval churches is apparent from around 1100, when there was a move towards a 'revival' of sorts for the Ionic capital, one which was also reflected in the design of newly manufactured pieces: from this time onwards we find churches furnished solely with Ionic capitals ❻ [75], ❽ [87]. These Ionic colonnades also grace church *atriums* ❸ [54] and the *porticoes* with which churches of this period were often equipped ❻ (pp. 146–147). The new or recycled Ionic capitals were usually combined with spolia shafts of plain, evenly coloured granite, although the individual columns could vary greatly in their diameter. The large number of contemporary capitals signals the coming of a new age, one which saw a return to the large-scale production of architectural elements.

Building on the past

T HE EARLY CHRISTIAN AND MEDIEVAL churches were not only built *from*, but also *on top of* ancient remains. There was nothing random about the sites chosen for new buildings. In the first centuries after the legalization of Christianity most churches were built outside of the city walls – hence the number of churches with the epithet 'fuori le Mura', which means just that. For one thing, in the first half of the fourth century the Christian cult (which forbade the practice of making sacrifices to the traditional Roman gods) was still such a thorn in the side of the old, pagan, ruling classes that churches had to be built on the outskirts of the city. And for another, and not least, it was important for the sanctity of the churches that they be associated with the graves of the saints and Christian martyrs. And since Roman custom dictated that all burials took place outside of the city and there had for centuries been a ban against moving the earthly remains of the dead, this determined where many churches were built. Today it is possible to visit several Christian subterranean cemeteries (*catacombs*), for instance those connected to the churches of Sant'Agnese fuori le Mura ❷ and Santi Nereo e Achilleo. It was not until the seventh-eighth centuries that a start was in some cases made on moving graves – or the bones and other relics they contained – over to the churches. Consequently, it then became more common to build churches in more convenient and sheltered spots within the city. In these churches, which may have been built on sites with no historical connection with Christianity, it mattered greatly that the building was founded on ancient or Early Christian remains in the form of saintly relics, which were usually embedded in the altar.

But there were also other heavily symbolic spots, apart from burial sites, on which churches might be built. Under many, if not most churches within the confines of the city, lie ancient and more or less anonymous, Roman buildings. Some of these underlying buildings may well have functioned as unofficial churches, *domus ecclesiae*, before the legalization of Christianity. When the building of churches became lawful and congregations grew so large that they could no longer be contained within ordinary houses, the tradition of the old place of worship was kept up by the building of a new church on top of it. In the course of time the name of the original owner of the old *domus ecclesia* often translated into the name of a saint, to whom the church was dedicated. In some cases these structures, which were filled with earth and rubble when the new church was built on top of them, have since been excavated and are now open to view. The present church of San Crisogono, which dates from the early twelfth century, sits on top of a fifth century church housed in a Roman *domus*; and the early fifth century church of Santi Giovanni e Paolo was raised on the remains of a *titulus* church established inside a Roman house in the fourth century. Under numerous other churches too, including San Clemente ❸, Santa Pudenziana and San Martino ai Monti, lie ancient Roman houses that are now open to the public.

During the Middle Ages some of the Early Christian churches gradually fell into disrepair, and the level of the streets also rose due to the steady accumulation over the centuries of earth, rubbish, silt from river floodings and much else besides ❸ (pp. 112–113). Occasionally an old building had to be demolished, but rather than rebuilding elsewhere the Romans of the High Middle Ages preferred to erect a new church on top of the old one. This explains the many historical architectural layers in San Clemente, where the upper church from the early twelfth century sits on top of the Early Christian basilica (c. 400). This in turn has been raised over a *mithraeum* (a temple to the Persian sun god Mithras) and a couple of other ancient Roman buildings, (first-third century) some part of which may have served as a church in the fourth century ❸ [**53**].

The building of a new church on top of an ancient pre-Christian temple can either be regarded as a sign of a desire to annexe the sacred power still associated with that particular site or as a way of erasing the memory of the rival cult. Christians were well aware of the observation, also formulated in rhetorical theory at the time, that if you want a building to be forgotten it is not always enough simply to tear it down. Because then people will only remember that *that* was where the building concerned had once stood. If, on the other hand, you erect a new building on the spot you blur and suppress the memory of its forerunner.

In many cases it was probably a bit of both, which is to say a desire to appropriate the sacred power and erase the memory of the rival faith. It is remarkable how effectively and systematically Christianity took over the rituals, religious festivals, imagery, symbols and functions of the older pagan cult. Our celebration of the birth of

Christ at exactly the same time as the winter solstice was once celebrated is just one of countless well-known examples of this takeover strategy. And it cannot be mere coincidence that several churches have been built on top of mithraeums. In Rome other examples of such over-building of Mithras sanctuaries, apart from San Clemente ❸ [53], include Santo Stefano Rotondo ⑪ and Santa Prisca. Worship of Mithras was widespread, especially in the third century and had, in fact, much in common with Christianity (or vice-versa). But although, with the benefit of hindsight, it does not look as if the cult of Mithras was ever a serious rival to Christianity, its influence was, nonetheless, strong enough for churches to be built on top of its sanctuaries.

It's interesting to note that in the first century after the legalization of Christianity there was a reluctance to convert older public buildings into churches. Not until the sixth century do we see documented examples of this practice, and then only secular

19 The so-called Temple of Romulus (post 307), which was probably an audience chamber for the city prefect. Under Pope Felix IV (526–530) the building was consecrated as the church of ❺ Santi Cosma e Damiano. The doorway, its frame of *porphyry* columns and the *lintel* with its hefty cornice are spolia and represent an early example of recycling in official Roman architecture at the beginning of the fourth century.

Building on the past

buildings of various sorts were selected for conversion – it would be a while longer before pagan temples were touched. An early example of such conversions is the 'Temple of Romulus' (post 307) in the Forum Romanum. Despite its name this was not, in fact, originally a temple, but most likely an audience chamber for the city prefect [19]. During the first half of the sixth century this building became part of the new church of Santi Cosma e Damiano. Another such example in the Forum Romano is the hall – probably the vestibule (second century) to the Imperial Palace on the Palatine Hill – which was converted, possibly in the 570s, into the church of Santa Maria Antiqua. These churches are also a sign that the whole city was now in Christian hands – the Forum Romanum was, after all, the official and religious hub of the Roman Empire. And the consecration by Pope Honorius I (625–638) of the church of Sant'Adriano, constructed within the seat of the old Senate itself, the Curia, in the Forum Romanum, was not lacking in symbolism. No one could now be in any doubt that the Church had taken control of Rome. That the building was dedicated to a saint who happened to be the namesake of the great emperor Hadrian (117–138) could on the other hand be seen as a striking mark of respect for the city's pre-Christian past.

After this hesitant start the practice of converting older secular buildings into churches became more and more widespread. Throughout the Middle Ages and right up to the Renaissance there are plenty of examples of such conversions, some more radical than others. Santa Maria in Cosmedin was built around 600 on the site of the *Statio Annonae*, the offices for Rome's public grain supply ❼ [79] [81], and as late as the second half of the sixteenth century Michelangelo was commissioned to construct the great church of Santa Maria degli Angeli in part of the Emperor Diocletian's *thermae*, an extensive baths complex from around 300.

There was, however, a marked resistance to the full or partial recycling of ancient temples. The earliest instance of this in Rome is the re-consecration of the Pantheon as the church of Santa Maria ad Martyres, also known as Santa Maria Rotonda, an event which occurred as late as 609, under the reign of Pope Bonifacius IV [20]. The Pantheon, as its Greek name suggests, had previously been dedicated to all of the ancient gods, but was now – with typical Christian sense for analogy, dedicated to all of the Christian martyrs. So in fact it wasn't until two hundred years after the legalization of Christianity (and its official acknowledgement, at the end

20 🔟 The Pantheon (consecrated as the church of Santa Maria ad Martyres in 609) in an old photograph from the mid-nineteenth century. Here one can still see the two towers from the 1620s, probably built by Carlo Maderno and Francesco Borromini. The towers were torn down at the end of the nineteenth century when greater priority was gradually being given to the buildings of ancient Rome than to the additions made in later Christian times.

of the fourth century, as the only lawful faith) that steps were taken to make new use of the Pantheon's formidable interior and unique structure. During the Baroque period two church towers were added to the building (torn down again in the late nineteenth century). Here, in the seventeenth century, it was obviously still felt – or possibly *again* felt, after the shock of Luther's Reformation – that the temple needed to look more Christian [20]. For centuries after the adaptation of the Pantheon to Santa Maria ad Martyres it was extremely rare for a temple to be reused as a church. The first definite example after the Pantheon that we know of is the little Temple of Portunus (often called the Temple of Fortuna Virilis) in the Forum Boarium, which was used as a church (Santa Maria Egiziaca during the papacy of John VIII (872–882). It was restored to its original temple form from its Renaissance modernization

21 **⑩** San Lorenzo in Miranda, constructed inside the Temple of Faustina in the Forum Romanum. The conversion to a church may have occurred as early as the seventh-eighth centuries, but the first proven documentation of this dates from 1192. The church underwent some modernization during the Renaissance and the Baroque era, which accounts for the present early seventeenth-century facade that lies behind the magnificent green-streaked *cipollino* marble columns of the *portico*. The interior of the building is seventeenth-century.

by Antonio Muñoz in 1925, while still preserving its ninth-century frescoes). Although there is a possibility that San Lorenzo in Miranda, constructed within the Temple of Antoninus and Faustina in the Forum Romanum, may date back to the seventh or eighth century, the first reliable record of the building as a church stems from the end of the twelfth century [21]. A last variation on the temple transformation theme can be seen in San Nicola in Carcere (twelfth century or possibly earlier), which has not made use of just one old temple, but in fact incorporates the remains of three temples that once stood here side by side ❾ [91].

Up to a point the scarcity of churches built *on top of* or *inside* temples can of course be put down to practical considerations. The traditional rectangular Roman temple with its relatively small *cella* was not particularly well suited to use as a church. Interiors as vast and splendid as the Pantheon's are the exception rather than the rule where Roman temples are concerned. But the gradual move towards temple conversions which started in the ninth century and was particularly prevalent in the eleventh and twelfth centuries, does show that whatever the layout of the traditional temples such transformations were not unfeasible.

The fact that temple conversions are so rare and were so late in coming is possibly a sign that Christianity needed time – needed in fact hundreds of years – to establish itself before daring to take on these buildings, which were still regarded as demon-ridden, idolatrous shrines. All in all, building on antiquity could present both an attractive proposition and a problem for Christian church builders. In the long run, though, respect for and the allure of Ancient Rome were probably the key factors in defining their attitude to the past.

Materials and meaning

I T IS SELDOM POSSIBLE to determine which buildings the spolia in Roman churches originally came from. In a few cases, however, architectural historians have detected similarities between spolia and various ancient buildings in the city and have thus been able to identify with reasonable accuracy the sources of the relocated pieces. So, in the splendid Santa Maria in Trastevere a number of the richly carved Ionic capitals in the *colonnades* of the nave hail from the early third century Baths of Caracalla ❽ [**89**]. The capitals of the columns on the façade of the Lateran Baptistery may have been taken from the Temple of Venus Genetrix in the Forum of Caesar ❶ [**37**]. This was a temple dedicated to the creative, life-generating powers of the goddess of love (as well as honouring Caesar's own line, since he claimed to be descended from Venus); and the *entablatures* crowning the façade of the Lateran Baptistery bear a close resemblance to those that can be seen to this day on the side wall of the Temple of Hadrian (mid-third century), which was rebuilt in the seventeenth century and converted into the city stock exchange in 1879 [**22**].

But ascertaining to what extent the materials for a spolia building were selected for the significance attached to their original locations is not that simple. In the examples mentioned above it could be argued that it made sense to use elements from the Temple of Venus Genetrix in a baptistery in which, as in the ancient temple, the focus is on birth and generation (through baptism). Likewise, it may have seemed only fitting to appropriate the prestige and the dignity associated with an Imperial temple – and one dedicated, what is more, to such a paragon as Hadrian – for a new Christian building.

But there were laws governing the preservation of distinguished public buildings, so the builders of new churches could not simply take what they liked from the city's ancient edifices or use them as they saw fit (see p. 22). To a great extent they had to content themselves with using the pieces that lay to hand in ruins and derelict buildings. And this imposed certain limitations. At the same time it seems unlikely, in an age when there was no such thing as architectural history or architectural criticism, that anyone would re-

22 The Temple of Hadrian (145) on the Piazza di Pietra. Rebuilt 1691–1700 and later. Since 1879 it has housed the city stock exchange.

member much about the origins of these pieces. It could be maintained, though, that such architectural elements possessed certain qualities – to do with their decoration, their finish, their proportions or material – which rendered them suitable for a particular type of building. In ancient Rome there was a great emphasis on 'decorum', as in 'what is right and seemly', and on adapting things to the given circumstances. The style and décor of a building were chosen to fit its purpose. One might, for example, choose very ornamental, slender, elegant pieces for a temple to a goddess, in keeping with the fundamental architectural analogies with the human body. A temple to a male deity, on the other hand, might be plainer, more monumental and robust in style. Even when removed from their original setting the inherent architectural qualities of these elements may well have been perceived and appreciated at an unconscious level, irregardless of whether their place of origin and its function had already been completely forgotten. So, the choice of the capitals from the Temple of Venus for the Lateran Baptistery need not have been determined by an interest in or knowledge of their origins. Perhaps the immaculate white marble and exuberant leafy ornamentation (which originally corresponded with the temple's procreative theme) simply seemed appropriate for a building of this type, in which an individual was born to a new life through the sacrament of baptism. The fact that architectural elements can clearly be invested with meaning and evoke associations that have nothing to do with a conscious knowledge or designation of them, is vital to the understanding of the spolia churches. There are indications that the materials and the way they were incorporated into the new buildings was deeply significant. If (as in Santa Costanza **❹**, Santi Giovanni e Paolo, Santa Sabina **❿** or San Martino ai Monti) twelve columns were used in a building, this in itself lent new meaning to the ancient pieces, as a metaphor for the twelve apostles, the pillars of the church, or as a symbol of the heavenly city of Jerusalem as described in the Book of Revelations, a description in which the number twelve is mentioned repeatedly.

The symbolism of numbers was taken very seriously at this time. But other numerals apart from twelve also played a central role in the churches, and not just when it came to counting columns: this focus on the metaphysical significance of numbers extended to doors and windows, to wall niches and to the actual structure of the building. Three, as in the three doors of a church, stood, for example, for the Holy Trinity, while eight symbolized the Resurrection, Christ having risen on the eighth day of his Passion. Generally speaking, the number eight was therefore an apt choice for Christian churches, with their promise of redemption after death, although it is perhaps found most often in those churches for which the tomb of a saint plays an important part, acting as it does as a reminder of the death and resurrection of the saint. So, in the crypt of San Lorenzo fuori le Mura the tomb of the martyr is surrounded by eight columns **❻** (p. 149). For the same reason the number eight held relevance for buildings such as baptisteries, in which baptism by (at that time total) immersion in water and the subsequent climb out of the water into life was a metaphor for the leaving of the old life and rebirth into the new, Christian life, with its message of redemption. The Lateran Baptistery is octagonal in form and the font is encircled by eight *porphyry* columns **❶** [**40**]. The number twenty-two, known from St Peter's [**11**], from Santa Maria in Aracoeli [**10**] and from the sum of the twin sets of columns in churches such as San Crisogono, Santa Maria in Trastevere **❽** and the Basilica of Honorius in San Lorenzo fuori le Mura **❻**, was regarded as representing the Old Testament, while the number twenty was interpreted as a symbol of the relationship between the Old and New Testaments. In San Paolo fuori le Mura, for instance, four rows of twenty columns separate the nave from the aisles, while two rows of twenty flank the nave of Santa Maria Maggiore (with another two columns added later). The sum of the two rows in San Pietro in Vincoli also added up to twenty [**15**].

This interest, so typical of the period, in the symbolic numerical approach to architectural features was not of course confined to number and form. It also extended to the fabric of the church. A porphyry column was not only admired for its distinctive purple colour. It also constituted a powerful metaphor for dignity and divinity. The attribution to the stone of these qualities dates back to late antiquity, when porphyry was used only for Imperial monuments, just as in ancient Rome the colour purple was a badge of rank, reserved for the upper echelons of society. Similarly, a highly polished marble surface was not merely technically impressive; with its reflective qualities and the durability and timeless perfection evoked by the smooth stone, it was of deeply significant symbolic and aesthetic value to the people of the Middle Ages, for whom light and infinity were the hallmarks of the divine. It is impossible to differentiate between aesthetics and meaning in medieval architecture. A material could not be 'beautiful' without also being 'good'. The idea of art for art's sake is a modern concept.

The elaborately carved, naturalistic foliage on a Corinthian capital from the 'classical' early Roman Empire also held significance for the people of the Middle Ages, whose contemporary imagery was abstract, anti-naturalistic and two-dimensional. They admired the ancient Roman architectural elements because they spoke of techniques and processes they no longer mastered and materials that were no longer available: porphyry, for example, had been imported to Rome in late Antiquity from one particular quarry in Egypt – but after the collapse of the Empire new products in this material were impossible to come by for centuries. Ancient stones (and works of art) were not always well-received, however, associated as they were with an age and certain values – e.g. materialism, rationalism, naturalism and physicality – which were abhorred.

This goes some way to explaining why ancient pieces were reused only up to a certain point, why elements were selected (or rejected) with care and why their original appearance was often modified by using pieces in new ways or in new combinations. Any reservations there might have been about ancient Roman architecture in general were dispelled by the break with tradition signalled by the spolia structures, in all their variety, with their mixtures of styles and materials, departures from standard patterns and classical proportions, the abolishing of the *column orders*, the combining of columns with arcades and so on.

The large number of small crosses one finds cut or carved into marble surfaces and columns in Roman churches ❶ [43] [44], ❺ [69], ❼ [86] may also be an indication that people were not always quick to accept the 'pagan' spolia'. Some of these crosses have been so roughly scratched that they seem in effect to be no more than graffiti scrawled there by pilgrims and other visitors in their religious fervour. But we also know that the dedication of new churches – and more particularly the re-dedication of ancient temples such as the Pantheon – involved a kind of exorcism ritual, to drive out any evil spirits. This ritual is not unlike that of baptism: buildings were sprinkled with holy water, anointed with the sign of the cross and so on – all to prepare them for their new Christian function. We can only assume that many of the crosses carved into the stones of the churches were inspired by the same thought and served the same purpose. They crop up everywhere: on a marble block used as a step, on floor tiles, on a doorpost, on pillars. Today, these are palpable signs that the materials themselves were not neutral or devoid of meaning. They could have positive qualities, but they could most certainly also possess a dangerous power which had to be neutralized before they could be used.

When building with spolia there may seldom have been a specific aim in using a particular element, one motivated by a knowledge of its provenance. Nonetheless the choice of such pieces can have been significant. Apart from the more obscure 'pagan' connotations with which the materials might be endowed, there was also an interest in understanding a building within a certain historical context. One simply has to look at the many legends about the churches of Rome that flourished in the Middle Ages. In this context it is irrelevant whether these legends have any actual basis in archaeological fact.

For example, in the old St Peter's were a number of quite unique spiral *Composite* columns in white marble, their shafts finely carved with vine scrolls. These columns, which are of Greek origin (first-third century) are known to have been an integral part of the church right from its foundation. The original six were, however, supplemented with six more in the eighth century (giving the evocative number twelve); the matching columns must have been discovered somewhere in the Byzantine Empire and duly taken to Rome. These spiral columns supported a *pergola* or decorative screen separating the chancel of St Peter's from the nave. Besides their beautiful stone and fine workmanship these columns also had special symbolic

23 **21** The crossing of St Peter's with ancient Greek spiral columns set into niches in the balconies. These columns are relics from the old St Peter's where they were a feature of a *pergola* in the chancel from the church's founding. In the foreground, a corner of G. L. Bernini's bronze baldachin from the seventeenth century whose spiralling columns decorated with vine scrolls echo the Early Christian spolia on the balconies.

value, since their spiralling, vine-covered form fitted with the Biblical description of the columns in the Temple of Solomon. In the sixteenth-seventeenth centuries, when the old St Peter's was torn down and the new one built, it was decided to reuse these columns, which can now be seen in the niches above the four balconies at the intersection of the nave and transept; and Baroque sculptor and architect Gianlorenzo Bernini echoed their spiralling, vine-adorned shafts in his designs for the columns supporting his massive bronze *baldachin* at the crossing of the church [23]. As to the origins of these columns, early Medieval sources tell us only that they came from Greece. But the High Middle Ages pilgrim guide *Mirabilia Urbis Romae* (c. 1140) expanded somewhat on this story, stating that these twelve 'glass columns' came from the Trojan Temple of Apollo itself – a legendary and highly significant place.

In the sixteenth century the columns of St Peter's were believed (as stated by Giorgio Vasari) to have come from the Mausoleum of Hadrian, converted in the Middle Ages into the fortress of Castel Sant'Angelo. The outside of the cylindrical upper section of the mausoleum was originally wreathed with columns and it was these columns which were said to have been "translated" to St Peter's. It is hard to say how much truth there is in the legend. But the fact that the shafts of the columns in St Peter's are of very different types of stone suggests that they did not all come from the same building [11]. It would be an appealing idea, though, for Christians: to think that the great basilica dedicated to St Peter – who was, according to the Gospel, the rock on which the Church was built – included pieces from the great Roman emperor Hadrian. As far as they were concerned the Church of Rome was the heir to the Empire – with the same power and status as Ancient Rome, but also now with the right faith.

It is not really surprising that Roman building materials were much sought after also outside of what is now known as Italy. In the 530s the Emperor Justinian is said to have taken columns from the Temple of the Sun in Rome for the vast church of Hagia Sophia which he built in the seat of the Eastern Roman (Byzantine) Empire, Constantinople. For one thing the sun god seemed a fitting precursor to Jesus Christ, who also epitomized light, for another it seemed only right that the new capital – 'The new Rome' – should be built from or founded on the stones of Ancient Rome.

There are many similar examples illustrating how ancient building materials were regarded as relics of great religious or political significance. Even in village churches in Denmark we find excep-

24 Fjenneslev Church on the Danish island of Zealand, with granite columns which may be spolia imported to Denmark in the twelfth century. There are several examples in Danish churches of granite columns which were in all likelihood brought there from abroad. The Danish art historian Otto Norn has suggested that they might have functioned as relics of a sort as well as providing ballast for ships returning from pilgrimages to the Holy Land. The capitals and bases date from the time of the church's construction.

tionally fine polished granite shafts which may well have been imported – not necessarily from Rome, but possibly from the Holy Land [24].

A couple of the most famous episodes in the history of spolia importation occurred in ninth-century Aachen and twelfth-century Paris: the great leader of the Carolingian empire, Charlemagne, set out single-mindedly to take possession, both literally and figuratively, of Roman civilization. He 'assumed' the title of Roman Emperor, having himself crowned in Rome in the glorious year of 800, and he imported Roman learning and imagery, not to mention art and building materials, to his court at Aachen in an effort to endow his empire with the authority of Ancient Rome. The grand Palatine chapel at Aachen (late ninth century) contains ancient columns acquired in this way – albeit imported not from Rome itself but from Ravenna. Ravenna in northern Italy was an important town which, in late Antiquity, had acted for a while as capital of the Western Roman Empire. It was the Roman pope – one who had, as it happens, chosen to take the notable imperial name of Adrian (Hadrian) I (772–795) – who gave Charlemagne permission to take these columns. Both of these great cultural and political figures have obviously been well aware of all the connotations and significance inherent in Roman stones and Roman heritage being used to grace the new empire's northern European capital. So the conceptual and concrete appropriation of ancient remains could take many forms. Pope Innocent II (1130–1143) arranged to have himself buried in a porphyry sarcophagus which, it was claimed, had originally held the body of the Emperor Hadrian. And from twelfth-century Paris we have reports testifying to the admiration for pieces of Roman origin. In the 1140s the powerful Abbot Suger from the Abbey of St Denis on the outskirts of Paris kept a record of the work involved in building a magnificent new chancel for his church – often described as the first Gothic building. In this he writes of how at one point he had considered getting hold of some enormous columns he had once seen in 'Diocletian's Palace' (the *thermae*) on a visit to Rome. Interestingly enough this was at exactly the same time as Innocent II was using building materials from Caracalla's Baths for Santa Maria in Trastevere in Rome ❽ [89] and having Santo Stefano Rotondo reinforced with the addition of two columns of such vast dimensions ⑪ [104] that they too could well have come from Roman baths. Suger explains that his plan did not come to anything, however, because he had instead 'miraculously' found the

Materials and meaning

25 Column inscribed with the words 'ACVBICVLO AVGVSTORVM in ⑬ Santa Maria in Aracoeli (latter half of the thirteenth century) [**10**]. This column is the third in the left colonnade, counting from the entrance. The inscription looks antique, but it was probably made at the time of the church's construction or later, in the fifteenth century, since it alludes to a popular medieval legend. The inscription suggests that the column comes from the imperial bedchamber: a most appropriate connection for a church which, according to legend, was founded on the spot where the Virgin Mary and the infant Jesus appeared to the Emperor Augustus in a vision.

necessary architectural elements only a short distance away from the building site in France. But whether he did seriously consider importing columns from Rome or not, his report attests to the high regard shown by people of the time for Roman building materials. The implication in his account is that the final result was far more impressive than it would have been had he used real Roman columns.

Where many of the legends that have circulated on the origins of certain spolia are unlikely to have any basis in historical fact, there are some cases in which the pieces themselves tell us where they came from: namely, those spolia that have been inscribed. In San Nicola in Carcere (eleventh century or earlier) there is one such column bearing an early medieval inscription (seventh or eighth century) ❾ [**95**]. This column originally stood in an older church and in its new position in San Nicola it became a sort of relic, endowing the later medieval church with all the authority of the early Middle Ages.

Another inscribed column can be seen in Santa Maria in Aracoeli [**25**]. The capital letters give the words 'ACVBICVLO AVGVSTORVM' the appearance of a genuine ancient inscription. This reference to 'the bedroom of the Augustuses' is highly significant since, according to medieval legend, Christ appeared to the Emperor Augustus in a vision on the spot where the church was then built. It is hard to explain why the ancient Romans would have written on a column in this way. So the inscription must be a medieval or Renaissance, imitating ancient script. Such an inscription was of great importance to the church because the column's purported imperial origins kept the link with the legend fresh in people's minds. Thus the column became a memorial.

But inscribed columns of this sort are rare. Inscriptions are most often to be found on the floors of the churches. The patterned marble floors are constructed out of recycled materials: columns that have been sliced up, all manner of marble panels, gravestones or other blocks bearing inscriptions and dedications from ancient buildings [26]. Such epigraphs were very common in ancient Rome, where both construction and renovation work was advertised by

26 Part of the floor in San Giovanni a Porta Latina (twelfth century). Constructed out of recycled marble, including fragments of gravestones and the like complete with inscriptions. The floor is inlaid with pieces of white and coloured marble such as green and red *porphyry* and *giallo antico*.

Materials and meaning

27 Wall display of ancient fragments: **20** the cloisters of San Paolo fuori le Mura. In Rome the custom for displaying spolia in this way dates back to the fourteenth-fifteenth centuries.

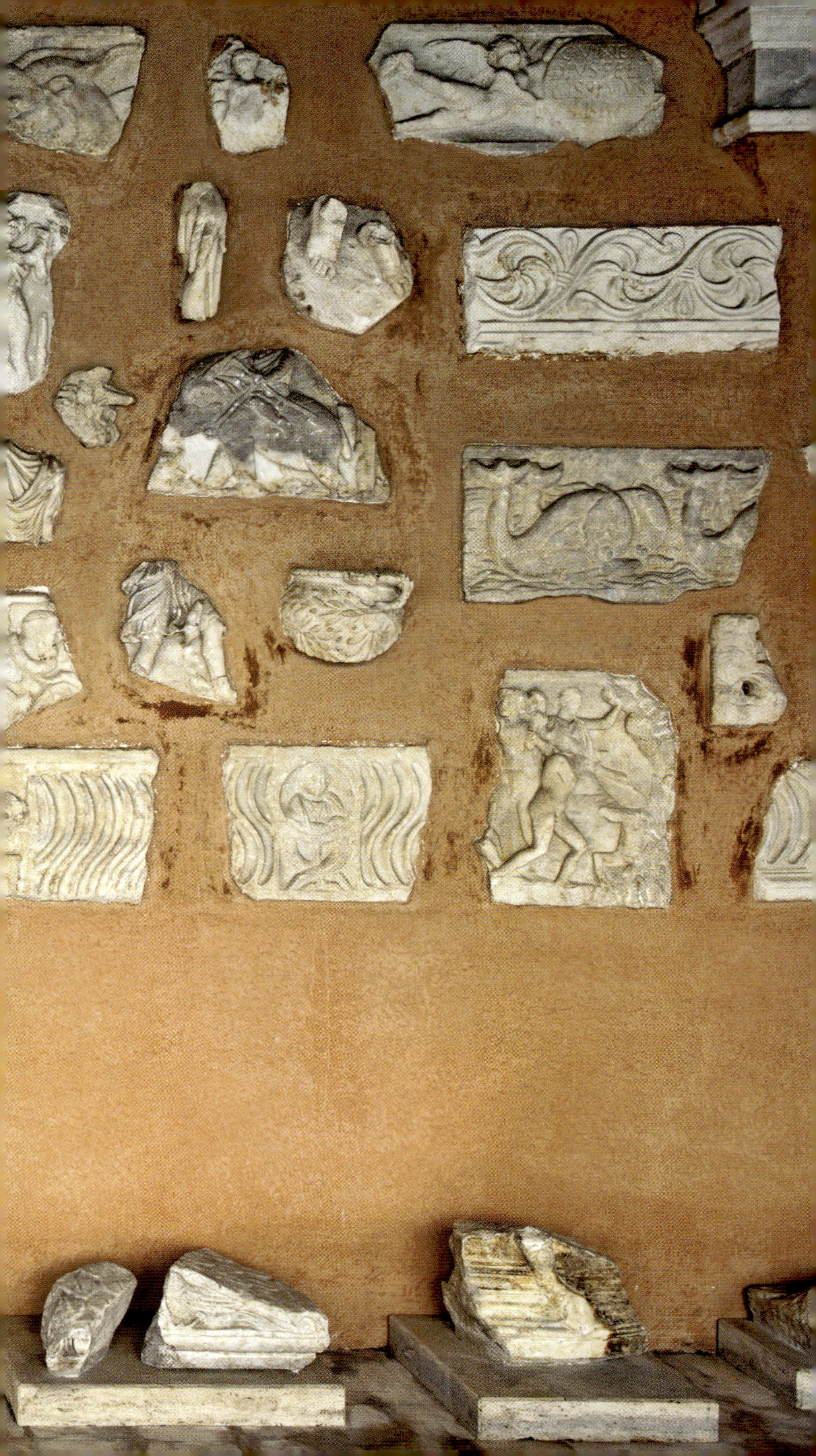

plaques on the walls of the buildings. In those cases where inscribed marble panels were reused, the builders could have placed them face down if they preferred not to have to look at these frequently pre-Christian writings. But they did not. Wherever you look in medieval churches – or those from around the sixth to the twelfth centuries at any rate – you see inscribed stones set in very conspicuous places on the floors ❸ [59], ❼ [83]. This does not necessarily mean that they were meant to be read: the plaques have often been cut in such a way that the writing too has been carved up into disjointed fragments, and a great many people were also illiterate. But the action of treading something underfoot is highly symbolic, speaking of subjugation and rendering harmless. We know from Early Christian, Eastern Roman sources that one could desecrate especially sacred, pagan pieces by using them as floor tiling – "that it might be trodden under foot not only by men, but also by women and dogs and swine and beasts" (Marcus Diaconus, c. 420, on the destruction of the Temple of Zeus in Gaza). But with the general respect for the ancient past that was so prevalent in Rome, it might be more reasonable to construe the floors as a very literal image of the church's founding on 'the old world' – whether this meant the Early Christian church and its martyrs, and the associations with these which the gravestones evoked, or simply ancient Rome in general, with all of its considerable clout. Here too one could conclude that it is a bit of both: on the one hand the church may have been seen as

28 Renaissance fountain featuring a combination of a mask set in a scallop shell and a granite trough from ancient *thermae*. Piazza Pietro d'Illiria outside ❿ Santa Sabina.

having destroyed the ancient, pagan religion and the floor tiling as a symbol of victory over tainted structures. On the other, the builders may have recognized the value of the church being built upon the authority and sanctity of the past.

In a few (rare) cases it is possible to ascertain that an inscription on a floor has had positive connotations. In the thirteenth century addition to San Lorenzo fuori le Mura, the Honorius Basilica, there is a tile inscribed with the name 'CONSTANTI' **6** [**78**]. This church was built on the site of a building founded by the Emperor Constantine, a large U-shaped *funerary basilica* known as the Basilica Maior, which fell into disrepair after a new church, San Lorenzo's Pelagius Basilica, was built next to it in the late sixth century. It appears likely that at least some of the columns in the thirteenth-century Honorius Basilica came from the old Constantinian basilica [**75**] along with some and perhaps much of the marble used for the floor. This does at least seem a probable source of the tile bearing Constantine's name. The very fact that this new church was built from and upon the first Christian emperor's stones and his name must have been positively charged. By reusing the inscribed tile the builders established a discreet spot commemorating the Early Christian founder and ensured that the new church rested on the right Early Christian foundations.

The special Roman fondness for ancient remains in general and the integration of these into new buildings in particular is also evident in the tradition for embedding all sorts of sculptural and architectural fragments, epigraphs, gravestones and sarcophagus reliefs in the walls of church *narthexes* **8** (pp. 174–175) or cloisters [**27**]. These tokens of a bygone age, which turned up just about anywhere one stuck a spade into the earth, were given a new lease of life as ancient or Early Christian stone collages: constant reminders of the city's historic past and its antique identity [**28**], [**29**]. It is not possible to determine exactly when this custom began, but from the fourteenth-fifteenth centuries onwards it was practised and systematized to such a degree that spolia walls of this sort can seem like actual antique collections. In the eighteenth century it was the observation of this long established custom which provided the inspiration for the first comprehensive book on Roman spolia, written by Giovanni Marangoni (1744). The floor tiling in the medieval churches and the common practice of embedding inscriptions and sculptural fragments into the outer walls of churches is the direct forerunner of these collages.

AM FORMA ENASO
PRO FORT AR ME
AB VRB CON M M C

VS AE D POS

DROGHERIA

ENOTECA
BETE AVON
CHALAV ISRAEL

29 The house of Lorenzo Manilio, its façade adorned with imitation ancient inscriptions (dated to the year 2221 after the founding of Rome, which is to say 1497) and ancient reliefs. 1–2 Via Portico d'Ottavia.

Old and new side by side

THERE WAS NO SHORTAGE of respect in Rome for the past. As we have seen in the previous chapter, the handling of the ancient stones could not simply be put down to an attempt to denigrate the pagan legacy – far from it. In other parts of the Early Christian world, however – especially in the Eastern Roman Empire – a more aggressive attitude towards ancient remains prevailed. From here we have accounts of temples being burned down and pagan architecture desecrated.

In Rome, though, you have to search a bit to find instances of spolia being used in ways that directly overturn and thus degrade the ancient pieces or 'subject' them to a new, Christian set of rules. It is rare here to see, for example, capitals inverted and used as bases, as one finds elsewhere in the area formerly covered by the Roman Empire. There is, however, a typical Roman example of this in Santa Maria in Cosmedin: here a capital has been used as the base of one of the columns in the nave, but it has been recut, so it is not easy to discern its original function **7** [**83**]. In other instances in Rome of upturned capitals being used as bases one has the same sense that practical and material considerations lay behind the choice of these pieces for this purpose [**30**].

This does not, however, mean that ancient spolia were always employed in the 'correct' classical fashion. On the contrary, in fact: as we have also seen, in pretty much every case the builders made greater or smaller adjustments in their uses and in the setting together of different materials, in order to achieve a result that would look very different from the ancient original. When column shafts or capitals of different finishes and colours are ranged side by side in one colonnade, and when the columns are released from their ties to the ancient *entablatures* and are combined instead with arcades, a very clear break is made with the ancient 'classical' tradition. And again, when a relief that once served a very different purpose is used as a door *lintel* in Santa Sabina this speaks of an unorthodox, anti-authoritarian approach to the legacy of antiquity **10** [**98**].

Although the use of spolia could therefore be a sign of renewal and 'improvement' of the ancient architecture, this does not mean that the citizens of medieval Rome wished to suppress or eradicate the memory of the past. This self-same juxtaposition of old and new was a highly significant feature of spolia architecture. The duality in terms of age lent to the churches by their recycling of ancient elements paralleled the relationship between the Old and New Testaments. To Christians, the Old Testament was not something that had simply been rendered redundant and obsolete by the birth of Christ. Instead the New Testament was regarded as the fulfilment of the Old. Throughout the Middle Ages there was a deep preoccupation with the way that episodes from the Old Testament foreshadowed events in the New Testament – the branch of theology known as typology. Generally speaking, the comparison of old and new constituted a leitmotiv in the theological writings of the time. Most remarkable, perhaps, from our point of view is the fact that the juxtaposition of old and new in architecture was also seen as a metaphor for Adam vis-à-vis Christ or the Old Testament vis-à-vis the New (Paulinus of Nola, early 5th century). Just as the Old Testament was not only repeated, but also echoed in the New, the spolia churches embodied an appealing duality, containing as they did old pieces employed in a new and improved fashion. The practice, from around the fifth century, of decorating the walls above the colonnades in the nave with mosaics or frescoes depicting typological pairings of scenes from the two Testaments was a figurative counterpart to the physical duality inherent in the rows of spolia columns.

Significantly, the number twenty-two, which symbolized the Old Testament, or – even better – the number twenty, which represented the relationship between the Old and New Testaments, were re-

30 Capital recut, inverted and used as a base in the porch of **23** Santa Prassede (thirteenth century), the old entrance to the church in Via San Martino ai Monti.

Old and new side by side

flected in the colonnades in several churches from around the year 400 onwards. This was at a time when murals depicting scenes from the two Testaments were also becoming popular (see, for example, Santo Stefano Rotondo **11** or Santa Maria in Aracoeli **13**). Thus, spolia architecture can have held special importance for the early Christians due to its incorporation of numbers relating to the Old and New Testaments and the setting it provided for illustrations of these. Such symbolic aspects were just part of a more widespread tendency at that time to regard the physical, tangible reality as a metaphor of a higher reality or truth.

The use of spolia was not merely a reflection of a superficial fondness for variation. The people of the Middle Ages did not differentiate between the appreciation of materials and aesthetics and the penchant for investing everything with meaning. Architecture was a metaphor: an analogy for something else, something greater. So it is also unlikely that medieval builders chose spolia purely for

31 **23** The Chapel of San Zeno, Santa Prassede (817–824). Ancient spolia in the form of black *porphyry* columns with entablature (third century) combined with 'pseudo spolia' (ninth century) consisting of bases and capitals.

Old and new side by side

their physical qualities, with no interest in – or possibly not even any thought for – whether the pieces in question were old or not. Nonetheless, in articles on art history dissertations one often encounters the assertion that individuals in medieval times possessed no sense of history. Not only that, but that they perceived themselves as living in an extension of antiquity, as if the past carried on into an endless present. This is true to the extent that they did not go around referring to themselves as 'medieval' (this patronising term, meaning literally a 'middle age', was first coined later in the Renaissance). But where spolia are concerned it is nevertheless fair to say that Christians did distinguish between past and present, between the pagan empire and the age of Christianity.

In San Lorenzo fuori le Mura, for example, in the old part of the church (the late sixth-century Pelagius Basilica), where a distinct break occurs in the pattern of ornamented marble beams forming the trabeation running across the columns, this could be interpret-

32 Detail of the door of the San Zeno Chapel [**31**]. The capital, the inscribed lintel and the carvings on the underside of the trabeation date from the church's construction in the ninth century.

Old and new side by side

ed as a sign of a deliberate intention to show that the church was constructed out of old elements ❻ [72]. And over the centuries it became more and more common to combine elements of different styles and materials – often pieces which had quite obviously not started out life together: for example, capitals that were larger or smaller in diameter than the columns on which they rested ❶ [41] ❹ [63] ❼ [84].

At the same time in the Middle Ages it was not unusual for 'pseudo' spolia to be produced, in cases where, for whatever reason, a particular antique piece was wanted, but was not readily available. As part of his wide-ranging cultural policy, in 800 Charlemagne imported not only columns (see p. 65), but also bronze sculptures from Ravenna and Rome for his new imperial capital of Aachen. He then swelled the numbers of these ancient sculptures – which were part of his campaign to consolidate his position – with newly manufactured pieces. These 'reproductions' were designed to act as stand-ins for original ancient Roman sculptures which it had not been possible to import to Aachen from the Italian states. In Rome an example of this can be seen in the ninth-century Roman church of Santa Prassede where an ornamented door-frame and Ionic capitals and bases from the time of the church's building were added to the spolia door of the San Zeno chapel [31]. These new elements were produced in the same style as the ancient columns and spolia entablature (third century); not only that, but the original unadorned underside of the beam was furnished with a decoration of stylized leaves [32]. When the church was built the hope was probably that these ninth-century additions would be regarded as 'genuine' spolia from ancient times, the respectful wish being to carry on the tradition of the Early Christian church.

So although the result achieved by building with spolia was quite unclassical – and typically medieval – there was also an interest in reproducing or manufacturing copies of the ancient prototypes. And it is worth noting that when Pope Bonifacius IV decided to consecrate the Pantheon as a church at the beginning of the seventh century (see p. 52) all that was required to make this arch-pagan Roman temple acceptable as a Christian house of God was an elaborate consecration ceremony and a new name.

It is, not least, this constant interplay between mistrust of the past and respect for it, faith in progress and the urge for renewal that makes the medieval recycling of ancient architecture such a fascinating and enigmatic subject.

Old and new side by side

I T IS DIFFICULT to gain a proper overview of the medieval use of spolia due to the many periodic phases of rebuilding, restoration and modernization that the churches have undergone – or been enriched by – over the centuries. The following guide to eleven selected churches may help visitors to make sense of what they are presented with in these buildings. Particularly drastic alterations were made to the churches after the Renaissance, in the seventeenth and eighteenth centuries, when the neo-classical architectural ideals of simplicity, classical proportions and 'proper' adherence to the ancient *column orders* really began to make themselves felt. The Counter-Reformation also led to modernizations [**33**] [**34**] [**35**]. Builders were not as yet hampered by our own day's museological sentimentality and insistence on preserving old buildings in some sort of 'original' state. And while they had considerable respect for the past and appreciated the religious and ecclesiastical worth of the Early Christian basilicas they preferred a more contemporary style of architecture. When it was decided to modernize the Lateran Basilica for Rome's jubilee year in 1650, Borromini suggested preserving the old basilica in its entirety by simply encapsulating it in a new shell (p. 31). According to the original designs there should even have been some oval openings high up in the new walls of the nave, offering glimpses of the old walls – "like a jewel set in a ring" as it was so beautifully put. In the end, though, these opening were covered by paintings. The uniform modern look took precedence over the ideologically founded aim: that the old Constantinian walls contained within the new ought to remain visible.

It is not only the modernizations of the seventeenth and eighteenth centuries that make it difficult to detect the original medieval elements in the churches. The same applies, not least, to the restoration work carried out in the nineteenth and early twentieth centuries, when additions made during the Renaissance and the Baroque period were often peeled away in an attempt to restore a church to the way it had first looked. In fact, though, churches then ended up bearing more resemblance to the nineteenth-century image of the Middle Ages, than to their original architectural form. Many of those churches which look modest and 'medievally' simple, with no visually overpowering Baroque altars and chapels (San Giorgio in Velabro **5**, Santa Maria in Cosmedin **7**, Santa Sabina **10**), were completely stripped and reconstructed in the nineteenth and twentieth centuries. As a result they now present an appearance which they never had and which is more akin to the spare, clean-

Old and new side by side

lined spatial ideals of Modernism, from which these restorations have sprung, than to those of the Middle Ages. Not that this detracts in any way from their appeal. One simply has to remember that what one is seeing is a historical reconstruction. Originally, in the Middle Ages when the walls and the sides of the apse were adorned with mosaics of gold and vibrant coloured glass or with huge frescoed murals they would have looked very different – brightly-hued and dancing with colour and light.

Most of the city's churches have, though, managed to retain much of the ornamentation with which they were furnished over the centuries. This too means that one sometimes has to do a bit of hunting in order to find the spolia, bombarded as the eyes are by the refurbishments of successive ages. But they are there. Most of the old churches in the city feature recycled elements of one sort or another. So if you would like to follow the traces of Ancient Rome all you have do is get out there and start looking.

33 PREVIOUS PAGES: **23** Santa Prassede (817–824). With spolia columns and entablatures in the nave and mosaics around the double *triumphal arch* and in the apse from the time of the church's construction under Pope Paschal I in the ninth century. But Santa Prassede was also thoroughly modernized (frescoes, coffered ceiling, stuccowork on entablatures and capitals etc.) in the late sixteenth century and early seventeenth century.

34 BELOW: Entablature in Santa Prassede where the stuccowork was removed in the nineteenth century to reveal the original, patchwork ornamentation underneath. The capitals on the other hand are nicely uniform thanks to the stucco added during the early Baroque era (c. 1600).

35 RIGHT: one of Santa Prassede's spolia capitals, stripped of stucco in the twentieth century.

Old and new side by side

CONSTANT

Selected Spolia Churches

Opening times given here are only a guideline. These may vary depending on the time of year.

Numbers in square brackets [1] refer to illustrations. A number inside a red circle ① refers to the description of one of the eleven selected spolia churches, a number inside a blue circle ① refers to one of the other noteworthy spolia churches listed at the end of this book, in the section on Practical Information. The red and blue numbers also indicate the locations of the churches on the maps at the front and back of the book.

Noteworthy nearby churches: Here you will find a list of other important spolia churches in the area. The eleven selected churches are numbered in red and given in bold type ①. Those numbered in blue ① feature in the list of other noteworthy spolia churches.

The descriptions of the church interiors and directions to left and right should be read from the point of view of someone standing with their back to the entrance, looking down the church. The first pair of columns in a church is that closest to the entrance. Movement around the church goes in a clockwise direction, so descriptions start with the right side/right side-aisle.

The Lateran Baptistery (c. 432–440)

or San Giovanni in Fonte
Piazza di San Giovanni in Laterano
Open: 7.30–12.30 + 16.00–18.30

THE LATERAN BAPTISTERY (San Giovanni in Fonte) is the baptismal chapel of the Lateran Basilica, Rome's cathedral, which was founded by the Emperor Constantine on a site next to the imperial Lateran Palace (p. 13). Constantine also founded the Lateran Baptistery. But it was completed in its present form during the reign of Pope Sixtus III (432–440). During the seventeenth century the Baptistery was restored and modernized several times, particularly under Pope Urban VIII (1623–1644). The building's ten *porphyry* columns (two on the façade and eight inside) are said to have been collected by Constantine himself. It is not known, however, whether the shafts of these are spolia from older buildings or whether they were in fact stock items, since new architectural elements in porphyry were still being manufactured and imported during Constantine's day. Apart from its very fine structural elements the Baptistery also contains beautiful and historically important fifth- and seventh-century mosaics in the apses of the *narthex* and the adjoining chapels.

In keeping with the great contemporary interest in numbers and their significance the Baptistery's octagonal form and the eight porphyry columns inside it were meant to symbolize resurrection and the promise of this inherent in the ritual of baptism.

The exterior

This small octagonal building was built partly over the remains of the bathhouse (*thermae*) of a Roman villa and of another fourth-century building. It is fronted on the south side by a *narthex* (access – by request – through the manned entrance to the right of the Baptistery), the doorway of which was once framed by a couple of *fluted* Corinthian pilasters in *pavonazzetto* marble (first century BC), though the one to the right has since been lost (pp. 86–87). The

---

Noteworthy nearby churches

- **7** San Giovanni in Laterano [**5**]
- **3** **San Clemente**
- **9** Santi Giovanni e Paolo
- **14** Santa Maria in Domnica [**18**]
- **28** Sancta Sanctorum
- **11** **Santo Stefano Rotondo**
- **26** Santi Quattro Coronati

door in the centre is flanked by two massive *porphyry* columns (their shafts made up of two sections) with Composite capitals (produced in Asia Minor, early second century) and exquisitely carved, richly ornamented bases of white marble (first century) [36] [37].

Porphyry itself was strongly associated with dignity and power: like purple garments the purple stone from Egypt was a symbol of status, and was reserved for emperors – used, for example, for imperial sarcophagi. Christianity borrowed these badges of grandeur and rank – the stone and the colour – from the emperor and assigned them instead to Jesus Christ. That columns made from such a heavily symbolic material are crowned by Composite capitals, with their apparent triumphal associations (the Christian triumph

36 Detail of the white marble base supporting the *porphyry* column to the right of the entrance (first century).

37 Detail of the entablature and Composite capital on the facade of the *narthex*. The capitals come from, or certainly resemble a type used in the Temple of Venus Genetrix in the Forum of Caesar. This entablature looks like that used in the Temple of Hadrian (the Rome Stock Exchange) (mid-third century) [**22**].

over death through baptism), can be interpreted as yet another indication, on the building's façade, of what lies within and of its function as a baptismal chapel [37].

These capitals resemble those in the temple to Venus Genetrix rebuilt in the Trajanic era (98–117). Little now survives of this temple, the rearmost inner chamber containing the Composite capitals is gone (not surprisingly, if the capitals were removed to another building). The remains of the temple stand in the Forum of Caesar, which was originally a venue for public and government affairs: a place with ancient Roman and pagan overtones which remained in use until the Christian takeover of the city at the beginning of the fifth century. If the capitals did come from there then the Christian builders of the Baptistery may have wished to make the point that the principles of renewal and procreation embodied in Venus Genetrix (the life-giving mother goddess) were now replaced by baptism, through which man was born into a new life. Whatever the case, it is fair to say that the materials which had originally been considered appropriate for a temple to Venus Genetrix must also have appealed to the builders who chose these elements for the Baptistery building (p. 57). This applies both to the exuberant leafy ornamentation and the triumphal connotations of the capitals.

Resting on the pilaster and the porphyry columns is an entablature very like the one on the Temple of Hadrian (mid-second century) on the Piazza di Pietra in the centre of the city (p. 57), which was first transformed into a palace and later, in 1879, converted into the Rome stock exchange [22]. Another section of the same entablature has been used inside the Baptistery [41]: an *architrave* (second-third century) doing service here as a trabeation. The large marble panels on either side of the door are later additions (as is the doorway itself): this side of the narthex was probably open or only screened by some sort of grille.

Note the various little crosses – probably 'Christianizing' marks – carved into the marble doorposts (see p. 61) [43] [44].

The interior

If it is not possible to gain admission to the Baptistery by the original entrance, through the narthex, visitors must use the newer entrance on the opposite, north, side of the building, from Piazza di San Giovanni in Laterano. This means cutting through the Baptistery to reach the narthex. One of the apses in the narthex is decorated with a magnificent mosaic of vines dating from the fifth

1

The Lateran Baptistery

38 The wall of the Baptistery *narthex*, showing the remains of the original *opus sectile* revetment: colourful marble mosaics from the fifth century.

century. On the wall to the left of the apse are the remains of a splendid ornamented marble *revetment* in *opus sectile* [**38**]. The walls of the octagonal central area – and of most other Early Christian churches – were originally decorated in the same way. The Baptistery consists of an *ambulatory* running round the eight porphyry columns encircling the font in the centre, which was designed for full immersion in water [**39**][**40**]. The columns are of varying thicknesses and heights, their differences evened out by capitals of different orders (and heights): two Ionic (second century), a couple of Corinthian (first century) and a couple of Composites (late second century) [**41**]. The columns were restored or, in the case of the Ionic pair, greatly remodelled in the seventeenth century and adorned with 'Barberini bees'. These bees are the symbol of the Barberinis, a powerful Roman family, one of whose scions was the man behind the Baptistery's refurbishment: Pope Urban VIII (1623–1644). The column shafts were restored and the bases replaced [**42**]. The columns support an entablature from the same source as the one over the entrance [**37**]. This has been carved up, in most unclassical fashion, into eight sections to fit the building's octagonal shape.

Ionic

Corinthian

Composite

All column shafts
of red porphyry

o   5   10 m

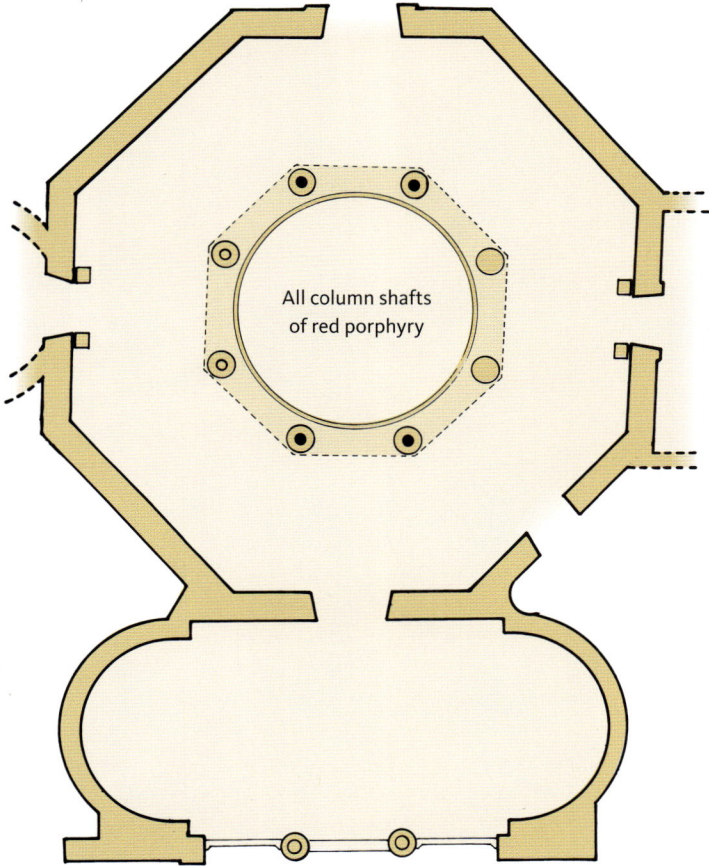

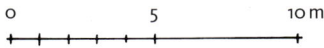

39 Floorplan of the Baptistery in its fifth-century form showing
the arrangement of the capitals.

EMINENASCITVRALMO
TVSEDITAQVIS

IMERCTREPECCATOASACROFVSCANTE
...VVTERHMAGDET...FARTVIIDMAS...H

40 The Lateran Baptistery
(c. 432–440)

41 Detail of the entablature showing one Ionic and one Composite capital. Note the similarity between the inner side of the entablature and the entablature used on the facade of the *narthex* [37] [40]. The only difference is that here the entablature is narrower because the smooth bottom band (*fascia*) has been sawn off. The outer side of the entablature has been furnished with an inscription from the time of Sixtus III. As can be seen most clearly on the Ionic capital, these capitals were originally made for narrower shafts.

It has also been shortened by the removal of the bottom bands (*fascia*) [41]. And, last but not least, the ornamented side – the ancient 'front' has been turned inwards to face the font. Pope Sixtus III had a series of verses on the sacrament of baptism inscribed on the undecorated, outward facing side; the assurance of rebirth contained in the last lines of the catechism on the west-facing section of the entablature chimes with the triumphal nature of the two Composite capitals on the west side.

Atop the porphyry columns stand smaller, white marble columns with Composite capitals, these last being seventeeth-century, bee-adorned replacements for the original spolia capitals. The chapel ceiling, ornamentation and wall paintings all date from restoration and modernization work carried out during the sixteenth and, more especially, the seventeenth centuries.

On the right-hand side of the ambulatory, just past the entrance from the narthex, is the entrance to the Chapel of San Venanzio (Cappella di San Venanzio) constructed by Popes John (640–642) IV and Theodore I (642–649) in an older column-borne building. The upper part of the end wall and the apse are decorated with beautiful mosaics from this period and on the wall on the left is a Corinthian *cipollino* column from the original building. On both the east and west sides of the Baptistery ambulatory are spolia door-ways leading to two chapels built by Pope Hilary (461–468). The door of the eastern chapel (Capella di San Giovanni Evangelista) is framed by porphyry columns with bases and Corinthian capitals of white marble topped by an architrave. Again, here, note the little crosses carved on the right-hand doorpost. These may have been put there when the chapel was consecrated or possibly later, in the twelfth century, when new bronze doors were installed. Or these could be less 'official' markings left there by centuries of pilgrims [44]. This chapel has an exceptionally early and beautiful vaulted mosaic ceiling from the fifth century. The door of the western chapel (Capella del Battista) is also flanked by trabeated porphyry columns, but here the bases and Corinthan capitals are of green porphyry (serpentine) and have been set on porphyry *plinths* [45]. The bronze doors here are the original doors from Pope Hilary's time.

42 Detail of columns showing clear signs of restoration to the shaft and a new base dating from the seventeenth-century renovation of the church.

43 Cross carved into the right-hand doorpost at the entrance to the *narthex* (see [**36**]).

44 Cross on the doorpost at the entrance to the Capella del Battista.

45 The Hilary Chapel (Capella del Battista) with porphyry columns supporting a marble trabeation. The bases and Corinthian capitals are of green porphyry (serpentine).

Sant'Agnese fuori le Mura (c. 625–638)

Via Nomentana 349
7.30 a.m.–12.00 noon + 4.00 p.m.–7.30 p.m.
Guided tours of the catacombs
9.00 a.m.–12 noon + 4.00 p.m.–6.00 p.m.
Closed Sunday mornings and holidays

SANT' AGNESE was built during the reign of Pope Honorius I (625–638) on the site of an earlier chapel to the martyr St Agnes and next to a large U-shaped *funerary basilica*, the ruins of which have been preserved, and an imperial mausoleum, now Santa Costanza ❹. All three buildings are reputed to have been built at the behest of one of Constantine's daughters, Constantina (died 354) during the years 337–351 (p. 126). She was later buried in the mausoleum along with her sister Helena. This particular spot was a significant one, lying as it did over an Early Christian subterranean cemetery (*catacombs*), and was therefore full of valuable relics. So Sant'Agnese is an *ad corpus* site, which is to say that the church is built over the remains of a saint – in this case the tomb of the martyred St Agnes. This also explains the church's distinctive location and its shape: since there was a reluctance to moving tombs, the church had to be built into the hillside in which St Agnes had been laid to rest (p. 49). This meant that the church also provided direct access to the large network of catacombs which, by the way, are very much worth a visit (entrance from the left side of the *narthex*). The church is rather like an oversized reliquary, covering and encapsulating as it does the earthly remains of St Agnes.

Exterior

The church, a typical red-brick building, is wider and taller than the usual style of basilica and also contains an upper gallery, reached through a door at street level next to the east-facing *apse* (pp. 100–101). Such galleries were not reserved for women, despite what their modern name *matronei* might suggest. This upper floor allowed the countless pilgrims eager to view the saint's tomb to circulate unhindered. There was no direct access from the gallery to the ground floor of the church which was entered instead by way of a flight of steps leading from the crest of the hill down to the church's south nave, where the present broad, sweeping marble stairway – a newer addition from around 1600 – now runs [**48**]. The main entrance on the church's west side was not established until 1603 in conjunction with the excavation of part of the hill on which the church sits. The inside stairway which now links the two floors is also a later addition.

Noteworthy nearby churches

❹ **Santa Costanza**, directly adjacent to Sant'Agnese

Interior

The simple seventh-century basilica was renovated by Pope Adrian (772–795) and over the centuries a number of chapels and side aisles have been added to it [47] [48]. The walls and ceilings have also been decorated with post-medieval frescoes. The baldachin or *ciborium* over the altar, too, is more modern (1614) while the four *porphyry* columns may have come from a medieval *ciborium*. Some features of the original church have however survived: in the apse is a beautiful seventh-century mosaic depicting Saint Agnes flanked, on the left, by Pope Honorius presenting an exquisite little model of the church and, on the right, (possibly) Pope Gregory the Great (590–604). Another original feature is the revetment of the apse wall with its grey-striped *Proconnesian* marble and purple vertical bands, like a stylized colonnade (the outermost bands even sport Imperial Corinthian pilaster capitals in bas-relief) supporting an entablature in the form of a horizontal porphyry band [46] (see similar panelling in San Giorgio in Velabro ❺ [68] and Santa Sabina ❿ [99]).

46 Detail of the revetment on the apse wall with panels of grey-streaked *Proconnesian* marble separated by vertical *porphyry* bands. The last band on either side is topped by a capital and functions as a pilaster supporting a horizontal porphyry band which serves as a stylized entablature.

2

Sant' Agnese fuori le Mura

47 Sant'Agnese, looking towards the apse (c. 625–638).

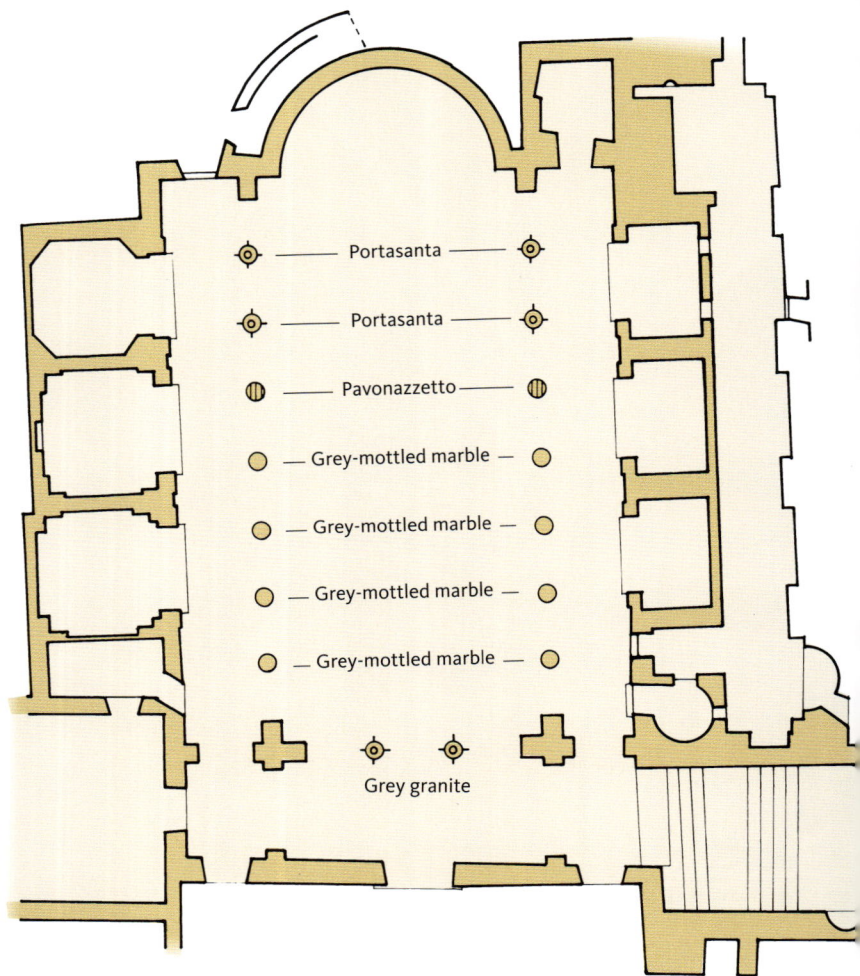

Portasanta — Portasanta

Portasanta — Portasanta

Pavonazzetto

Grey-mottled marble

Grey-mottled marble

Grey-mottled marble

Grey-mottled marble

Grey granite

○ Corinthian, smooth shaft
◐ Corinthian, fluted shaft
◑ Corinthian, spiral-fluted shaft
◈ Composite full-leaf capital, smooth shaft
⊛ Composite, fluted shaft
⊛ Composite, spiral-fluted shaft
▢ Impost capital

48 Sant'Agnese: plan of ground floor and galleries.

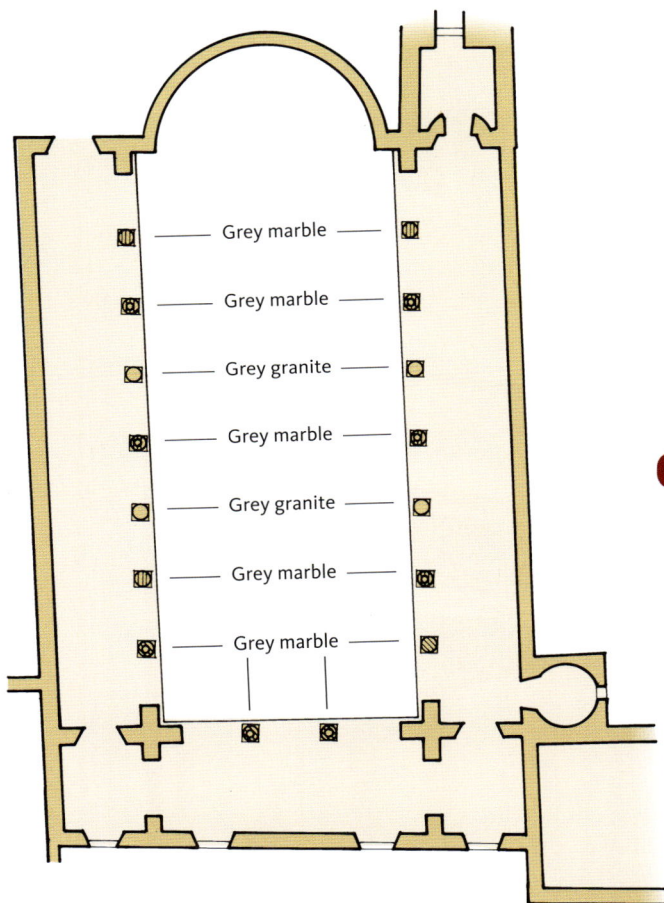

Grey marble

Grey marble

Grey granite

Grey marble

Grey granite

Grey marble

Grey marble

Sant' Agnese fuori le Mura

0   5   10 m

PAVLVS · V · PONT · MAX

49 The three last columns closest to the altar, probably indicating the area reserved for the clergy.

CRIPTA

CARD VERALLIVS

50 Sant'Agnese, looking towards the western end and the present entrance.

Sant' Agnese fuori le Mura

The church also contains a very fine and varied range of spolia in the form of columns and capitals in the arcades of the ground floor and the gallery, both of which are supported on each side by seven columns. The different elements are arranged symmetrically in pairs across the central axis of the church – a common layout, particularly in early medieval spolia churches [**47**] [**48**]. On the ground floor the four columns closest to the west wall of the church are of unpolished grey-mottled marble with Corinthian capitals from the time of the Roman Empire, while the fifth set consists of *fluted* columns in white, purple-veined marble (*pavonazetto*), though still with Corinthian capitals from the same period. The last two pairs are of a particularly beautiful red-veined, polished marble (*portasanta*) on which rest Composite full-leaf capitals (second century) [**49**]. Although these capitals are simply fashioned it has nonetheless been considered appropriate to place them closest to the church's *triumphal arch* and the altar, presumably due to the Composite order's particular triumphal associations – i.e. the Christian triumph over death. The nave seems to be split into two halves: the part closest to the entrance with its homogeneous matte-grey columns topped by identical Corinthian capitals and the section running down to the altar with its contrasting elements: white fluted marble with Corinthian capitals and gleaming red marble with full-leaf capitals. It seems likely that this arrangement was meant to accentuate the division in the church between the simple, uniform area designed for laymen and the grand diversity of the section reserved for the clergy, close to the altar (see p. 37).

On the ground floor, the nave is separated from the *narthex* by a triple-arched arcade supported by two grey granite columns with Composite full-leaf capitals [50].

In the gallery, grey and *pavonazzetto* marble shafts (fluted or spiralling) alternate with grey granite shafts (smooth) with Corinthian and Composite *impost capitals* from the time of the Roman Empire [48] [51]. The third and fifth pairs of columns are Renaissance replacements (fifteenth century). In the gallery too the columns are arranged symmetrically in pairs across the central axis. All except the first two pairs, that is. These four have instead been arranged in a crosswise pattern (Corinthian + Composite and Composite + Corinthian). The two columns on the west balcony have spiralling shafts of grey marble with late antique Ionic impost capitals [50].

The arrangement of the different elements has to be considered in the light of the way the first visitors moved around the church. The spiral shafts at the west end of the gallery may have been meant to indicate that this was the prime spot on this floor, offering as it did a clear view of the tomb. On the ground floor, on the other hand, where one entered from the right side aisle, the finest and most varied materials were situated closest to the apse.

51 The church's western/northern colonnade and gallery.

San Clemente

(c. 385–417 / c. 1099–1125)

Via di San Giovanni in Laterano/
Piazza di San Clemente
9.00 a.m.–12.30 p.m. + 3.00 p.m.–6.00 p.m.
Sundays and holidays: 12 noon–6.00 p.m.
Entry (by admission charge) to the
lower church and the Roman buildings
and mithraeum until twenty minutes
before closing time.

SAN CLEMENTE consists of three layers: a medieval church with an Early Christian basilica underneath it and below that again a layer of ancient Roman buildings. It is, therefore, a unique example of the way in which one age quite literally built upon the one before. The present upper church was erected in the early twelfth century, the lower church was constructed inside a third-century Roman building at the end of the fourth century and at the very bottom lies a Roman building from the second century (or earlier) with a *mithraeum*, added at the beginning of the third century [52] [53]. In San Clemente the name of the founder of the original parish church, *Titulus Clementis*, gradually 'translated' (as was often the case in the history of the Early Christian church) into that of his namesake, the early pope Clement I (88–97). Likewise, the church itself represents a quite literal 'translation' of older structures to a new function and a new significance. By building on top of the underlying mithraeum the early Christians were not only able to take practical advantage of some good solid foundations, they could also assume the significance, power and sanctity of the place – or obliterate its dangerous pagan associations by building over it. Both strategies are possible and the one does not preclude

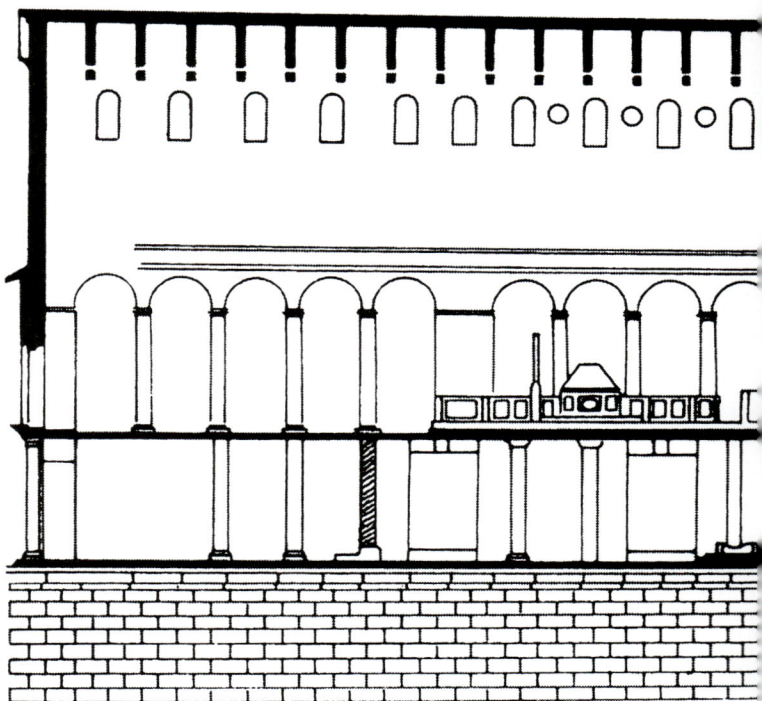

Noteworthy nearby churches

- **1** **The Lateran Baptistery** [5]
- **7** **San Giovanni in Laterano**
- **9** Santi Giovanni e Paolo
- **14** Santa Maria in Domnica [18]
- **28** Sancta Sanctorum
- **11** **Santo Stefano Rotondo**
- **26** Santi Quattro Coronati

the other (see pp. 50–51). Other churches in Rome – Santo Stefano Rotondo, for example **11** (p. 208), or Santa Prisca on the Aventine Hill – are also built on top of mithraeums. And this is probably no coincidence, since there were many similarities between Jesus Christ and the Persian sun god Mithras and at that time Mithraism posed something of a rival to the growing Christian faith. So the Christian appropriation and overbuilding of such sanctuaries made good sense.

San Clemente is also worth visiting for the sake of the magnificent mosaic in the *apse* of the upper, twelfth-century church.

3

San Clemente

52 San Clemente (c. 400 and c. 1100).
Cross-section of the building showing the two layers of churches and the Roman buildings bottom right.

53 *Mithraeum* from the beginning of the third century in the complex of Roman buildings on which San Clemente was built.

Exterior

In the late eleventh century the Early Christian church was in such poor condition (possibly due to the damage wrought during the sack of Rome by Robert Guiscard's Normans in 1084) that during the reign of Pope Paschalis II (1099–1118) Cardinal Anastasius (c. 1099–1125) had the present upper church built on top of it. Thus the lower church provided the foundations for the new building. During the late Baroque period (1713–1719) Carlo Stefano Fontana created a new entrance to the church on the Via di San Giovanni in Laterano. But the original twelfth-century entrance on the east side (facing Piazza di San Clemente) consists of a porch flanked by two pairs of antique columns, the front pair of granite with Ionic capitals, the back pair of *cipollino* (left) and granite (right) with Corinthian capitals (pp. 112–113). The doorway is framed by marble beams adorned with early medieval scrollwork. The lowness of the doorway in relation to the street provides a clue to the difference in levels between the new and the medieval city.

The atrium

The original eastern entrance of the upper church leads to an *atrium* (which can also be entered from the church itself should the original entrance on Piazza di San Clemente be closed) [**54**]. This atrium is the only well-preserved one of its kind from medieval Rome. The column shafts here are of grey (different shades) and red granite shafts together with a single grey-striped *Proconnesian* marble shaft. The capitals are mainly Ionic, either antique or twelfth-century reproductions (with a couple of modern replacements and a few exceptions from the Ionic rule: a simple Doric capital style in *peperino* marble and a couple of short Corinthian versions).

Interior: the upper church

The twelfth-century church was modernized by C.S. Fontana during the years 1713–1719 and the coffered ceiling, frescoes and stucco work all date from these renovations. The triple-naved basilica has eight columns running down each side of the central nave, each colonnade interrupted in the middle by a pier [**55**]. The shafts are of various types of stone – *cipollino*, different sorts of light and dark grey marble, *fluted* white marble, granite in red and varying shades of grey – and are arranged more or less in pairs across the central axis. During the eighteenth-century refurbishment the Ionic capitals on the columns were all made to match with the aid of stucco, although they do still vary in size. The bases also vary in shape and height to make up for the differences in the lengths of the shafts. The apse and the *triumphal arch* are decorated with a stunning mosaic (dating from the church's construction) which, with its vine motif, harks back to the mosaics we know of from the Early Christian churches (see the *narthex* mosaic in the Lateran Baptistery, p. 92). So what we have here is an adoption of an older artistic

3

San Clemente

54 *Atrium* with Ionic columns from the beginning of the twelfth century.

55 San Clemente. The upper church (c. 1099–1125).

tradition, a kind of figurative spolia. The church's *liturgical* accoutrements date from the twelfth century. These include the *ciborium* (albeit with sixteenth-century columns); the *Cosmatesque* floor (first decades of the thirteenth century, restored), inlaid with inscribed spolia stones (mostly gravestones), particularly in the right side-aisle; and in the centre of the nave a choir or *schola cantorum*, with a screen separating the choir from the rest of the church. This screen has been constructed partly out of materials from a similar earlier structure (first half of the sixth century) in the lower, Early Christian church. The marble panels are of *Proconnesian* marble, made in and imported from Constantinople.

In addition to the late Baroque frescoes in the church itself, the Capella di Santa Caterina boasts some fine early fifteenth-century frescoes by Masolino da Panicale.

The lower church

From the sacristy off the northern side-aisle of the twelfth-century church a flight of stairs leads down to the Early Christian basilica below, which dates from the final decades of the fourth century or the early fifth century. The excavation of the Early Christian church was begun in 1857. Till then its existence had been forgotten due to

56 Columns in San Clemente's lower church (c. 385–417): left side of the nave viewed from the entrance. The columns have been set into walls and vaulting built in more recent times to safeguard the underground chambers and reinforce the church built on top of them in the early twelfth century.

57 Columns in the *narthex* of the lower church: Pink marble (*portasanta*) and black marble.

the fact that during the building of the twelfth-century church the old basilica underneath had been filled in with earth and rubble. The stairs lead down to what was originally the *narthex* of the triple-naved basilica. This in turn leads to the main body of the church, which has been partially reinforced with more recent brick walls to provide a solid foundation for the upper church [56]. Here and there the brickwork has been removed to reveal the original columns at the entrance from the narthex and between the central nave and the side-aisles [57] [58] – two sets of eight columns featuring a wide range of shaft types, smooth and fluted, in different colours of marble. One of the shafts in the right-hand, northern colonnade may have been replaced in the seventh century. A few of the capitals are visible: they are a mix of Composite and possibly Corinthian full-leaf capitals (Roman, dating from the church's construction) together with one unusual cylindrical capital which may be an up-

turned base. Matching columns have not been organised in pairs, facing one another across the central axis. Instead they appear to have been arranged according to a more unusual principle: as a rule similar columns have been ranged in pairs within the same colonnade.

This church also contains some vestiges of the sixth-century *sectile tessellato* floor, inlaid with pieces of recycled marble slabs complete with inscriptions (mainly from Early Christian tombs). On the walls are the remnants of frescoes from several different centuries (eighth century onwards) painted during the days when the building still functioned as a church.

From the level of the Early Christian church a flight of steps leads down to the underlying structure: the third-century mithraeum and several rooms from a Roman building featuring the remains of some fine stucco ceiling decorations [**53**].

58 Column on the right-hand side of the nave: Green-mottled marble (*verde antico*) and Composite full-leaf capital.

59 San Clemente, the lower church. Floor from the sixth century inlaid with fragments of spolia marble complete with inscriptions (from gravestones and the like).

3

San Clemente

Santa Costanza (c. 337–351)

Via Nomentana 349
9.00 a.m.–12 noon + 4.00 p.m–18.30 p.m.
(Closed Sunday mornings and holidays)

SANTA COSTANZA was built as an imperial mausoleum (c. 337-351). It came to house the earthly remains of the daughter of the Emperor Constantine, Constantina (died 354) and her sister Helena. Constantina was laid to rest there in a splendid *porphyry* sarcophagus (the one on display is a copy, the original is in the Vatican Museum). She was later declared a saint and in the Middle Ages the building was duly consecrated as a church (first written mention of it as Santa Costanza in 865). The mausoleum was built next to and in connection with a large U-shaped *funerary basilica* (the ruins of the outer walls can still be seen) built above an underground cemetery (*catacombs*) [**60**]. These fourth-century buildings were supplemented by the present Sant'Agnese basilica ❷ in the seventh century. During the Middle Ages and the Renaissance the mausoleum was referred to as an 'ancient temple to Bacchus', but it has never served any such purpose. One reason for this post-antiquity association of the mausoleum with Bacchus, the ancient god of wine, could be the wine-harvest scenes depicted in two of the mosaics on the *ambulatory* vault and in the reliefs on the porphyry sarcophagus.

Exterior

The small central building is cylindrical, with a low main building and a tall central *tambour* which was originally crowned by a dome [**60**]. It was constructed, in typical Early Christian style, out of plain, unadorned brick, but when first built it was encircled by an external colonnade. Thus it harked back to the ancient Roman tradition for circular temples as well as pointing the way forward to what was to become common building practice in Early Christian times and the early Middle Ages: the exterior of the building is of plain stone, the columns moved inside to grace the interior. One salient feature of the church is the circle of twelve windows in the tambour, corresponding to the *clerestory* windows of Early Christian and Medieval basilicas, as seen, for example, in Santa Sabina ❿ [**99**]. The mausoleum has originally included a small *narthex* of which only parts of the side walls and their apse walls have survived (pp. 124–125) [**62**].

Noteworthy nearby churches
❷ **Sant' Agnese fuori le Mura**, directly adjacent to Santa Costanza.

60 In the foreground, the ruins of Sant'Agnese's original coemeterium or *funerary basilica* (c. 350). On the left in the background the church of Sant'Agnese **2**, on the right the mausoleum, now Santa Costanza (c. 337–351).

Interior

Inside, the church consists of a circular passage or *ambulatory* running round a high central space [**61**] [**62**]. The ambulatory has a barrel-vaulted ceiling beautifully decorated with mosaics dating from the building's construction (c. 350). The mosaics are executed as two identical sets of panels facing one another across the axis from the entrance to the apse, with a single cross-patterned panel above the entrance. The central dome was also decorated with fourth-century mosaics, but these have been lost and were replaced in the early seventeenth century by frescoes which have since also disappeared. Typically for their time these mosaics – which we only know of second-hand, from Renaissance drawings and descriptions – featured candelabra and vine motifs interspersed with small figures and scenes from the Old and New Testaments. The walls were originally covered with marble revetment reaching all the way up to the windows (as can still be seen today in some church apses, above the colonnades in Santa Sabina **10** [**101**] and in the *narthex* of the Lateran Baptistery **1** [**38**].

The ambulatory is separated from the central space by a colonnade in the same way that the side aisles are separated from the nave in the standard basilica. The twelve pairs of columns, which at first glance may look identical, are actually a discreet mix of spolia or stock elements. Column shafts of a different colour from the others

61 Santa Costanza (c. 337–351) looking from the entrance towards the apse with its imperial *porphyry* sarcophagus (a copy, the original is now in the Vatican Museum).

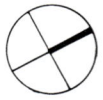

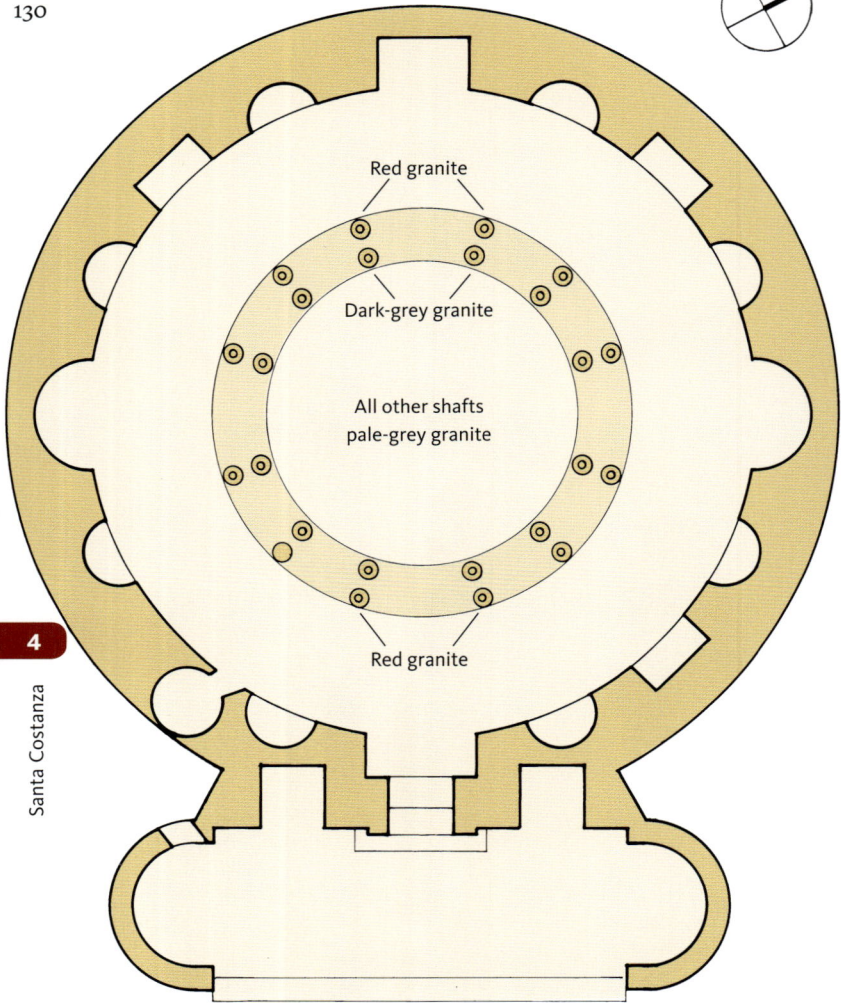

Red granite

Dark-grey granite

All other shafts
pale-grey granite

Red granite

◎ Composite

○ Corinthian

0   5   10 m

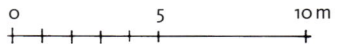

62 Floorplan of Santa Costanza.

have been used to define a central axis: the two columns directly opposite the entrance in the outer circle are of red granite, as opposed to the other matte, pale-grey shafts (granito della Troade). And on the other side, in the columns farthest away from the entrance, not only do we have two red granite shafts in the outer circle, in the inner ring are a couple of dark-grey, polished granite shafts (granito del Foro) [64]. The arcade opening thus highlighted provided the setting for the imperial *porphyry* sarcophagus. These arcade openings are, moreover, slightly wider than the rest, accentuating the longitudinal axis, from the entrance to the apse, as well as the transverse axis, thus hinting discreetly at a cruciform composition. The combination of the cross shape, which is repeated in the mosaic over the entrance, and the twelve pairs of columns, which could be seen as representing the twelve apostles, has probably been regarded as a concrete illustration of the building's Christian nature. Another of the motifs in the barrel-vaulted ceiling and on the sarcophagus – the grape-harvesting 'putti' or cherubs – can likewise be construed as a new, Christian reference to the Eucharist, although these images can also be regarded as classic Bacchanalian scenes. During the fourth-century transition from the old, pagan Roman civilization to the new Christian culture such suggestions and ambiguities were more the rule than the exception. In the niches of the 'transverse axis' are early medieval apse mosaics featuring images of Christ, greatly restored in 1843. The age of these mosaics is debatable: they may date from as far back as the second half of the fourth century.

The space is defined still further and the impression of a hierarchy reinforced by the use of two different sets of Composite capitals. In the inner circle an elaborate set of capitals from the time of the Emperor Augustus (early first century) have been used, while the outer circle contains smaller, somewhat later and less intricately carved capitals from the Severan perod (c. 200/ early third century) [63]. This marked the progression from the ambulatory up

4

Santa Costanza

63 The two types of Composite capital: on the left the outer, more modest Severan form (c. 200/early third century); on the right, from the inner circle: a large, ornate Augustinian version (end of first century BC). The shaft and capital of the left-hand column did not originally belong together, hence the difference in their diameters.

64 The two pairs of columns supporting the arcade at the top of the central axis in Santa Costanza and fronting the apse containing the sarcophagus. The outer columns are of red granite, the inner two are of dark-grey, polished granite, contrasting with the other unpolished, pale-grey granite shafts in the circle (see for example the two columns on the far right).

to the holy of holies, which is to say the central space under the light-filled, originally mosaic-adorned and hence colourful and reflective dome.

Although this is an imperial building, its construction has evidently not only involved the use of recycled elements or stock pieces selected and combined with a great deal of thought and care, in order to achieve variety rather than homogeneity of form. Great emphasis has been placed on subtle variations in colour and decorative detail.

So it is particularly interesting to note how one capital in the outer ring stands out from all the rest: a single Corinthian piece breaking the run of Composite capitals [65]. It is hard to imagine that the builders could not have got hold of one last Composite capital in the same style as the rest if they were aiming for a uniform effect. The church as a whole perfectly exemplifies the way in which its builders employed delicate and subtle variations in texture, finish and tone. It seems likely, therefore, that they deliberately chose to insert this one capital of a different order. Positioned as it is, as the last (or the first, depending on which way one moves around the ambulatory) column before the pair flanking the entrance to the church, it may have functioned as a marker, indicating the end of the circular colonnade – a visual full stop – before the entrance.

The capitals of each pair of columns are topped by a so-called *impost block*, a reference to the entablature which traditionally ran across the columns in Roman architecture. As with the exterior, the building's interior epitomizes a kind of hybrid or transitional phase, between the traditional approach to the columns as carriers of a horizontal trabeation and what was to become the new solution in Early Christian architecture: the columned arcade. Viewed from the front the columns appear to be linked to an arcade; viewed from the side they seem to be carrying an entablature [61]. The columned arcade, a beautiful, early version of which can be seen in Santa Sabina ❿ [99], was later to become the most popular option in the Middle Ages.

65 The last (or first – depending which way round one walks) couple of columns to the west of the entrance, with a Corinthian capital in the outer circle as opposed to the Composite capitals crowning all the other columns.

San Giorgio in Velabro

(c. 827–844)

Via del Velabro 3

10.00 a.m.–12.30 p.m. + 4.00 p.m.–18.30 p.m.

SAN GIORGIO IN VELABRO has a simple, tranquil interior, stripped of all post-medieval ornamentation in the 1920s (by Antonio Muñoz). This lovely little church provides a fine illustration of ninth-century spolia use in all its rich variety. It is one of many that sprang up during that period around the Forum Romanum, the political and religious centre of ancient Rome. In this way the Christian city promoted its counterpoint to the ancient customs and beliefs. San Giorgio in Velabro sits close to the massive Arch of Janus (fourth century) and abuts onto the smaller Arco degli Argentari (Arch of the Moneylenders, 204) with its exquisitely crafted reliefs: a striking example of the mix of historical periods in which the city abounds.

Exterior

With its modest scale, its *campanile* (eleventh-twelfth century) and its *portico* this brick-built church is not unlike the nearby Santa Maria in Cosmedin ❼. The portico was rebuilt early in the thirteenth century, using contemporary Ionic capitals resting on spolia shafts of *cipollino*, white marble and grey granite (restored after a bomb attack in 1993) and carrying an architrave. The entrance to the church is beautifully framed by antique marble beams.

Interior

The triple-naved basilica is built on the remains of an older building and this goes some way to explaining its irregular, slightly trapezoid layout and the fact that the side-aisle on the right is wider than that on the left [66]. The eight columns running down each side support an arcade [67]. The *clerestory wall* which in medieval times was decorated with colourful frescoes is now plain and unadorned after the restoration of the church in the 1920s, during which the Baroque decorations were removed in a typical historicist attempt to endow the church with an 'authentic' medieval appear-

Noteworthy nearby churches

❷ San Bartolomeo all'Isola
⑬ Santa Maria in Aracoeli [10]
❼ **Santa Maria in Cosmedin**
❾ **San Nicola in Carcere**

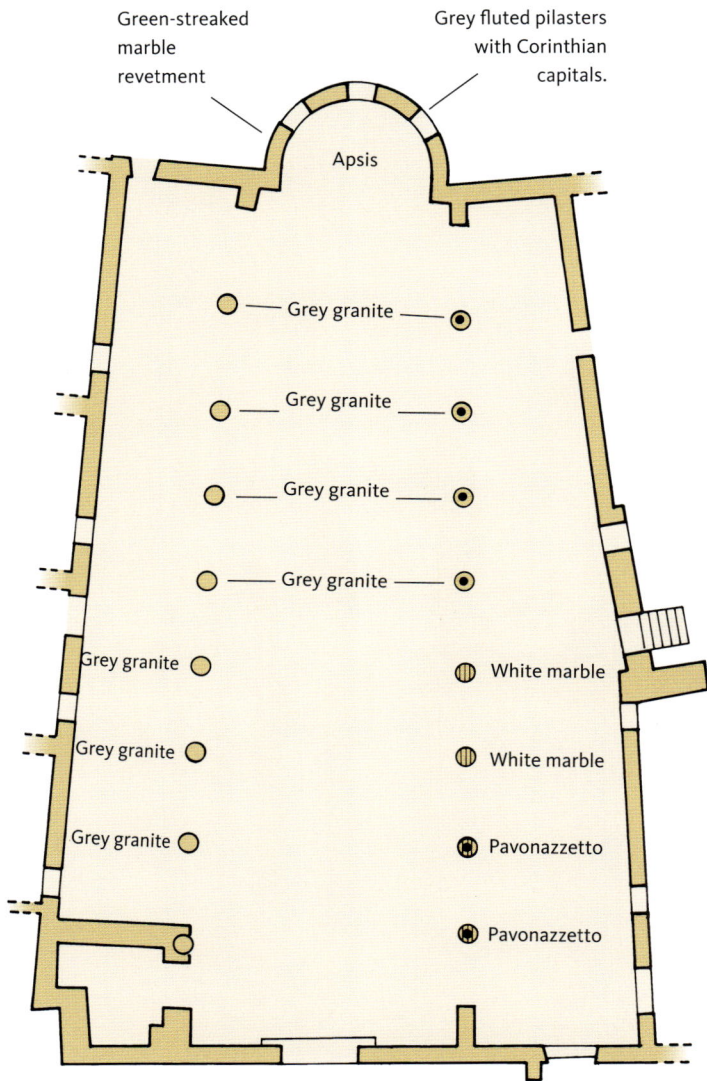

Green-streaked marble revetment

Grey fluted pilasters with Corinthian capitals.

Apsis

Grey granite

Grey granite

Grey granite

Grey granite

Grey granite

White marble

Grey granite

White marble

Grey granite

Pavonazzetto

Pavonazzetto

San Giorgio in Velabro

5

⊙ Smooth Ionic shaft
⊛ Fluted Ionic shaft
○ Fluted Corinthian shaft
▥ Fluted Corinthian shaft

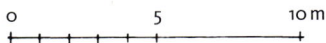

0   5   10 m

66 Floorplan of San Giorgio in Velabro.

67 San Giorgio in Velabro, looking towards the apse (c. 827–844).

ance. In the apse are frescoes which may echo the original mosaics. These frescoes, which date from the late thirteenth century, are credited to Pietro Cavallini, but were repainted in the sixteenth century. Preserved on the wall of the apse are panels of original – though restored – marble revetment (of the sort found also in Santa Sabina **10** [**99**] and Sant'Agnese **2** [**46**]) of green-streaked marble separated by grey-veined, *fluted* pilasters with Byzantine-Corinthian capitals (sixth century).

The church's *ciborium* is from the twelfth century (the four marble columns supporting the baldachin are replacements from the late eighteenth century). The chancel has a beautiful *Cosmatesque* floor from this same period, constructed as was usual out of recycled marble fragments (the circular tiles, for example, are cut from ancient columns).

The common practice of arranging matching columns in pairs, facing one another across the longitudinal axis of the nave has not been followed in San Giorgio in Velabro. Here there is no accord between the two sides of the church. The first column on the left side has a pale-grey marble shaft, but all seven that come after this have shafts of grey granite. All of the shafts in this colonnade are topped by Corinthian capitals, albeit of different styles (first – fifth/sixth century). The first two columns on the right-hand side, however, have fluted *pavonazzetto* shafts with matching Ionic capitals (first century?), then come two white, fluted marble shafts with matching Corinthian capitals (first century?) and finally four smooth, grey granite shafts with Ionic capitals: the first two of these are simple in design, from the late Early Christian period; the last two, closest to the apse, are slightly more ornate and are probably of ancient Roman origin.

The differentiation between the right and the left may have been intended to reflect the *liturgical* tradition of separating the sexes in church, with the 'good' side on the right designed for the male members of the congregation and the left side reserved for the female members (see p. 37). It is interesting to note that the side presenting the most homogeneous collection of elements was not necessarily regarded as being the more attractive side. Quite the opposite, in fact. Monotony was associated with the (in Latin quite literally) 'sinister' left side, while the diversity of form and materials on the right was to be prized and admired. It is also interesting to see how exquisite elements such as the fluted antique marble

68 The apse of San Giorgio in Velabro, panelled with green-streaked marble and grey-veined Byzantine-style pilasters (seventh century).

columns are positioned at the beginning of the nave and not closest to the apse as was often the case in early churches. Instead the
colonnade ends, at the entrance to the apse, with the more modest
Ionic granite columns. This may have been due to a desire to link
the area closest to the altar with the virtues of humility and poverty: Christian ideals which have regularly been emphasized throughout the history of the Church as reflections of Jesus Christ's own
humility and material poverty. If this area was reserved for the
clergy, then the four simple, austere granite Ionic columns may well
have been an indicator of this.

Note the crucifix carved into the centre of one of the steps up to
the chancel. The marble block used for this step has been marked
with the sign of the cross to 'Christianize' or consecrate it for Christian use, either at the time of the Church's construction or more
probably while still in its original location [**69**]. Elsewhere, small
double crosses have been etched into the steps on the left and in the
marble tiling in the nave. These may also have been signs of Christ-
ianization, or they may simply be marks left by pilgrims or other
ardent Christians.

The level of the floor in the nave and side-aisles was raised in
1601, but was lowered again during the restoration in the 1920s.

5

San Giorgio in Velabro

69 Cross carved into a step
in the chancel of the church.

San Lorenzo fuori le Mura

(c. 578–590 / c. 1216–1227)

Piazzale del Verano 3

7.30 a.m.–12.30 p.m. + Winter: 3.30 p.m.–7.00 p.m. /
Summer: 4.00 p.m.–8.00 p.m.

SAN LORENZO FUORI LE MURA is one of the smaller, but also one of the most beautiful and most undisturbed of Rome's seven main pilgrim churches. It has a quite unique interior, combining, as it does the naves from two different churches, one from the sixth century and one from the thirteenth [**75**]. It sits in the Campo Verano cemetery, a spot which has been used as a burial ground since Late Antiquity: first in the form of *catacombs*, later as a basilica-style cemetery similar to the original Sant'Agnese *funerary basilica* from the fourth century [**60**]. Spolia columns or stock elements were employed in the construction of this so-called Basilica Maior by the Emperor Constantine (or his family) during the first half of the fourth century. Archaeological excavations have revealed that it lay very close to the present church – parallel with and to the south of it.

Great significance was ascribed to the presence of saintly relics in or underneath the altars of Early Christian churches. But due to a reluctance in the early centuries of Christianity to moving the earthly remains of saints, the churches were instead built over the graves. So, like Sant'Agnese (2), San Lorenzo was built into the side of the hill where the cemetery still lies: *ad corpus*, which is to say over the grave of St Lawrence himself. It is only in more recent times that the eastern end of the church has been dug free of the catacomb hill. Originally, entrance to the church was via the south-facing side-aisle, with another doorway on the hilltop leading to the galleries above the nave.

The western end and the entrance were bombed in 1943 and rebuilt in the latter half of the 1940s.

Be sure to visit the church's fine, late twelfth-century cloisters. The adjoining Santa Ciriaca catacombs are currently closed for renovation.

Exterior

In 1220 the church's western façade was furnished with an elegant *portico*, credited to the architect and sculptor Vassalletto (pp. 146–147). This portico features examples of the beautifully fashioned, newly manufactured trabeated Ionic capitals which were typical of thirteenth-century Roman architecture. Of the six columns, the outermost on either side are of dark-green marble, the next two are *spiral-fluted*, *pavonazzetto* columns, while the two in the middle – also spiral-fluted – are of white marble. To the right of the church is a *campanile* from the twelfth century.

Interior

The inside of the church consists of two parts: the older, eastern section facing the catacomb hill, with its entrance to the galleries, is the so-called Pelagius Basilica, built during the reign of Pope Pelagius II (578–590) [**70**]. The newer, western section, known as the Honorius Basilica, houses the nave entered from Vassalletto's portico, which was added to the original church during the reign of Pope Honorius III (1216–1227) [**75**]. At that time the apse wall of the Pelagius Basilica was knocked down to allow Honorius's new nave to extend into the old basilica. The mosaics high on the wall at the western end of the Pelagius Basilica testify to this wall's original function as a *triumphal arch*. On the left in the row of figures depicted in the mosaic is Pope Pelagius II presenting a model of the church. So when the thirteenth-century extension was added the orientation of the church was reversed: the Pelagius Basilica became the chancel of the new composite church.

The church was restored in the 1860s under Pope Pius IX (1846–1878) by Virginio Vespignani, who removed the ornamentation added during earlier centuries, in order to restore the church to its 'pure' medieval appearance.

The Pelagius Basilica

The original small but lofty church with its galleries has much in common with Sant'Agnese ❷ and both are *ad corpus* churches with altars located over the graves of their respective saints [**70**]. Galleries are a rare sight in Roman churches, but in the Pelagius Basilica, as in Sant'Agnese, this feature made it possible for crowds of pilgrims to circulate around the building, taking in the saint's tomb in the body of the church.

In the thirteenth century, when the Pelagius Basilica was converted into the chancel of Honorius III's vast nave, the floor of the old church was raised. But during the modern restoration the floor in the side-aisles was lowered again to its original level [**71**]. The right-hand side-aisle is entered through a gate (enquire in the sacristy). The crypt containing the tombs of St Lawrence and two other saints is on the same level as the original side-aisles. These are surrounded by eight marble columns (a suitably symbolic number for a tomb, see p. 59): four of *verde antico* marble, two of dark-grey marble – all of these with medieval Ionic capitals – and two slender white marble columns from around the year 1200.

70 San Lorenzo fuori le Mura.
The Pelagius Basilica, looking west (c. 578–590).

71 The columns in San Lorenzo's Pelagius Basilica, seen from the side-aisle. The columns in the foreground are Corinthian with *fluted* shafts. The farthest away column, next to the church's original triumphal wall, has a distinctive figural capital and a shorter, *half-fluted* shaft.

At the far end, in the area originally occupied by the *narthex* of the Pelagius Basilica, is the Chapel of Pope Pius IX (1882–1895), is an exuberant example of mosaic work based on historicist ideas of medieval mosaics. From the side-aisles one has a floor-to-ceiling view of the five spolia columns on either side of the nave [**71**]. The first four pairs of columns (from the eastern end of the church, towards the catacomb hill) are of fluted *pavonazzetto* with their original capitals (second century). The last pair, (from the Severan era, c. 200/early third century), which flank the original *triumphal arch* – which is to say, the wall that was removed in the thirteenth century to open up the Honorius Basilica – are smaller and shorter than the others. They have therefore been placed on high *plinths* decorated with a crucifix relief (from the time of the church's construction) [71]. These two columns also differ from the other four pairs in their colour, being of white marble; in finish, with their distinctive *half-fluting*, and in the style of their capitals: they are crowned by figural capitals carved with 'trophy' reliefs, which is to say, reliefs depicting the spoils of war in the shape of the enemy's armour, weapons and the like [72]. Reliefs of this sort may originally have adorned a Roman triumphal arch or victory monument. Reused here in San Lorenzo they have been translated into a quite different kind of triumph, namely the Christian triumph over death – a significance accentuated by their position which, in the church's original sixth-century form was the most exalted of all spots: closest to the triumphal arch, the altar and the apse.

From the raised floor in the nave of the Pelagius Basilica one can take a closer look at the capitals of this last pair of columns [70] [72]. In contrast to the combination of columns and arcades so frequently found in Roman medieval churches, these columns support a trabeation pieced together from several different marble blocks (second and third century). The reliefs on these blocks reveal that some of them (for example those with reliefs on the underside) have originally served as doorposts, friezes and the like [73]. So this is not a classic entablature of the sort that the spolia columns must

72 Two columns – one featuring a figural capital carved with 'trophy' reliefs, the other with a Corinthian capital – supporting a trabeation patched together from sections of differently ornamented marble beams.

73 Part of the trabeation showing reliefs carved on the underside: evidence that these blocks were not originally part of an entablature.

have supported in their original location, one consisting of well-defined mouldings and made up of an architrave, frieze and cornice. Only the two Corinthian pavonazzetto columns marking the end of the nave bordering on the original narthex (facing the catacomb hill), which are part of the same set as those in the nave, support what could be called an appropriate, coherent and classically elegant entablature with a deep cornice [**74**]. The original entablature for the rest of the colonnade may have been in just as good condition as the columns, but the builders have chosen not to use it. It is clear that no attempt has been made to arrange the different blocks forming the entablature in such a way as to create a uniform effect. Quite the opposite, it seems. The way the elements have been put together highlights the area leading up to the original triumphal arch, the blocks here having been arranged two by two, 'mirroring' each other across the central axis of the nave – thus following the common practice of arranging elements in matching pairs, seen in the disposition of columns and capitals in the colonn-

ades of other church naves (see p. 32). The two rows of corresponding
columns flanking the western end of the chancel have followed the
(physical and spiritual) progress of worshippers up to the altar. The
patchwork effect of the entablature may have acted as a reminder
that there was talk here of spolia and hence that the church had
been constructed out of ancient stones, and not only that but
that those old elements had now been incorporated into a new and
better setting than their original 'pagan' surroundings, which were
so closely associated with the old Rome.

The galleries, in themselves, constitute another deliberately contrasting feature, with the columns here supporting arcades as opposed to the trabeation on the ground floor [**70**]. The two columns
closest to the original triumphal arch stand out from the rest in the
same way as the couple down below with their 'trophy' capitals: the
pair in the gallery have spiral shafts and Composite capitals, while
the four columns on either side of them are half-fluted and have
Corinthian capitals. Where columns one, two and three on the
left side and columns one and two on the right are of white marble,
column four on the left and column three and four on the right
are of pavonazzetto with more subtly defined fluting.

74 The eastern end (the original entrance wall) of San Lorenzo's Pelagius Basilica.

6

San Lorenzo fuori le Mura

75 San Lorenzo fuori le Mura: the Honorius Basilica, looking east (c. 1216–1227). In the background, the Pelagius Basilica (578–590) which now serves as the chancel of the composite church.

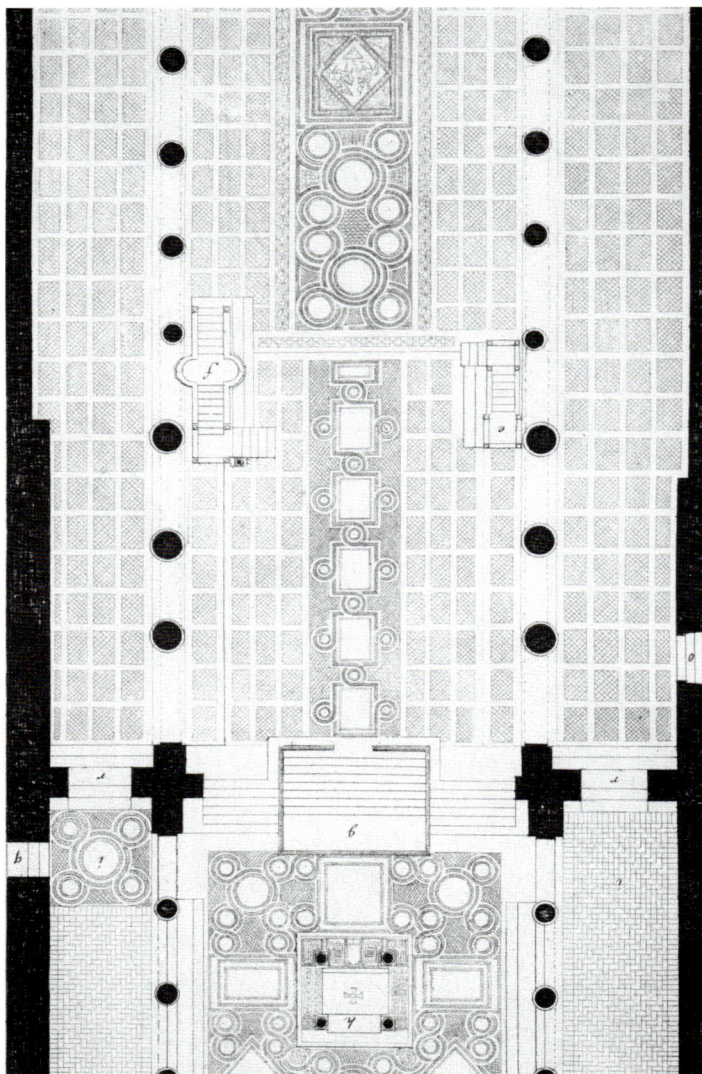

76 Floorplan showing a change in the tiling of the floor of San Lorenzo's Honorius Basilica, corresponding with the area originally reserved for the clergy. The columns are arranged in such a way that a particularly slender pair effectively frames and defines this area.

In the gallery at the eastern end of the church are three arches supported by two columns of black Egyptian granite with Byzantine Corinthian capitals from the fifth century or possibly from the time of the church's construction (i.e. imported at that time), set on marble plinths carved with crosses and birds [74].

The splendid *ciborium*, with its antique, Corinthian, *porphyry* columns and colonnaded, pyramid-shaped canopy is signed and dated 1148 (restored in the nineteenth century). The episcopal throne is from the thirteenth century, partly constructed out of older materials and featuring *Cosmatesque* work. The magnificent Cosmatesque floor dates from the first half of the thirteenth century.

The Honorius Basilica

During the reign of Pope Honorius III (1216–1227) the present nave was added to the Pelagius Basilica, which then became the chancel of the new, larger church [75]. Honorius's basilica was erected close to the by then derelict *funerary basilica*, the Constantinian Basilica Maior. The nave is lined by eleven pairs of Ionic granite and *cipollino* columns. These are arranged in pairs across the axis of the nave according to their size, which varies from very broad to slender shafts, and set on plinths of varying heights to compensate for the differ-

6

77 The eighth capital on the right-hand side of the Honorius Basilica is carved with a frog and a lizard, thought to be the 'signature' of the architect Vassalletto.

ent lengths of the columns. The shafts – all except the tenth pair – are arranged in pairs of the same stone: four pairs of grey granite, three pairs of cipollino, one pair (the eighth) of red granite and another (the ninth) of grey granite. The tenth pair consists of a grey granite shaft on the right across from a red granite shaft on the left. This is followed by another matching pair, in this case with shafts of grey granite. While some of the shafts may have come from the original Basilica Maior (which is known to have contained cipollino shafts), the bases and capitals were produced specially for the church and are thus typical of the Ionic 'revival' seen in Roman architecture around the year 1200. A change in the pattern of the exquisite thirteenth-century *Cosmatesque* floor is proof that the nave originally contained an area reserved specially for the clergy (what would later be known as the *schola cantorum*) [**76**]. This area has extended from the end of the nave abutting onto the Pelagius Basilica to the eighth pair of columns which, apart from being of red granite are also distinguishable from the others by their strikingly slender, short shafts set on correspondingly high plinths. The use, here, of such different elements has acted as an indicator of, or a frame for, this area's *liturgical* function.

The eighth column on the right-hand side also stands out from the rest, carrying as it does an unusual capital: this is the only capital in the church to be decorated with two small reliefs, one of a frog and one of a lizard [**77**]. There is an ancient legend (related in Pliny the Elder's *Natural History*) which tells of two Greek architects who 'signed' a column in this fashion and these reliefs in the Honorius Basilica are thought to be an allusion, inspired by this legend, to the architect Vassalletto, who designed this building: both a signature and an acknowledgement or assertion of the ancient culture and its significance.

Here and there on the floor one comes across recycled stone fragments carved with inscriptions. See, for example, the word 'CONSTANTI' inscribed on a tile in the right side-aisle, next to the sixth column. This has no doubt been prized both as a piece of spolia from the Early Christian basilica and as a reference in general to the first Christian emperor [**78**]. This tile is a good example of the discreet references often contained within recycled stones.

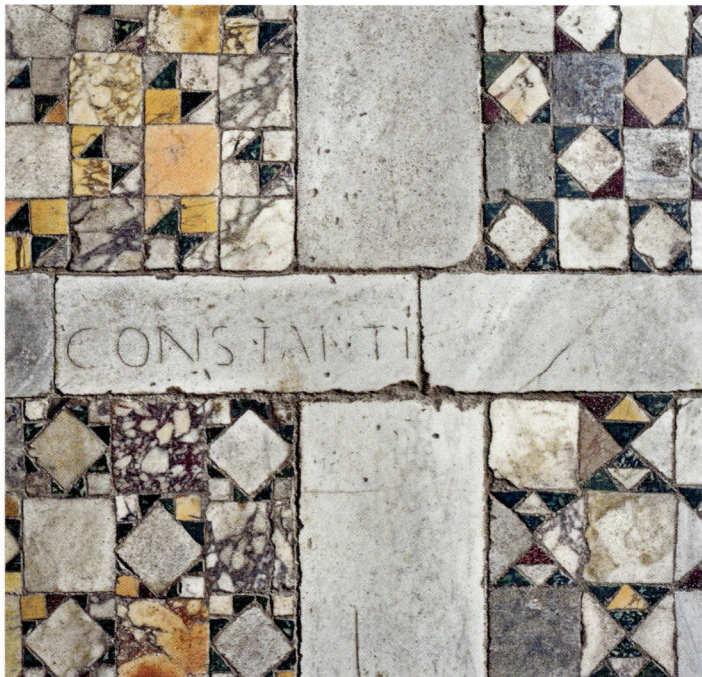

78 Tile on the floor of the Honorius Basilica showing the inscription 'CONSTANTI'. It was common practice for ancient inscriptions, Early Christian gravestones and the like to be incorporated into the floors of medieval churches. See also [26] [59] [83]. In many cases it is debatable whether these inscriptions were viewed in a positive or a negative light, since the very act of treading something underfoot was in itself heavily symbolic of suppression and denial. In some instances, where the inscriptions have been set into a wall, they have been turned upside down. On the other hand, the inscriptions also seem to have been valued as ornamentation or decoration. But when, as here, an inscription makes such clear reference to the Emperor Constantine who founded the first basilica on this spot, one can only assume that this tile was prized as a relic of sorts from the Early Christian building.

6

San Lorenzo fuori le Mura

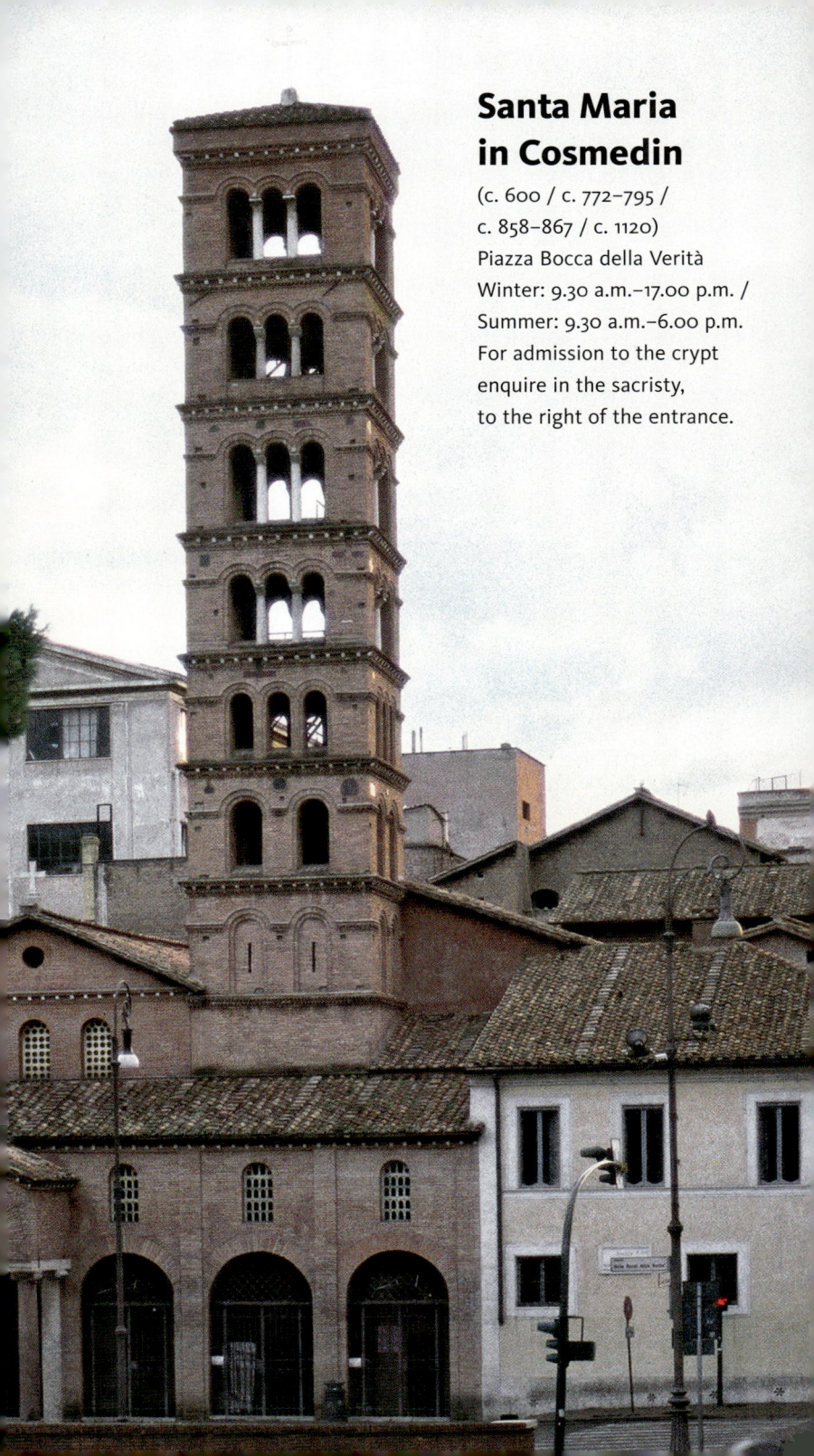

Santa Maria in Cosmedin

(c. 600 / c. 772–795 /
c. 858–867 / c. 1120)
Piazza Bocca della Verità
Winter: 9.30 a.m.–17.00 p.m. /
Summer: 9.30 a.m.–6.00 p.m.
For admission to the crypt
enquire in the sacristy,
to the right of the entrance.

SANTA MARIA IN COSMEDIN is a popular attraction for visitors to Rome. It is famed for the 'Bocca della verità' or Mouth of Truth, an ancient drain cover in the form of a stone face housed in its portico (legend has it that anyone who tells a lie while their hand is inside the mouth will have it bitten off), its dimly lit, atmospheric medieval chambers and its beautiful floor mosaics. It was constructed as early as the year 600 within a colonnaded *loggia* (fourth century), part of a complex of older buildings whose original function is the subject of some debate: one of them may have served some secular purpose, while another has been a monumental temple to Hercules, Ara Maxima Herculis [79] [81]. During the reign of Pope Adrian I (772–795) a thorough reconstruction and extension of the church was undertaken. Since it was used by the Greeks who had lived in this quarter since ancient times, it was given the Greek name 'Kosmidion', meaning ornate, due to the lavishly decorated interior. The fine little crypt underneath the church also dates from Adrian I's time. Again, during the reign of Pope Nicholas I (858–867) and in the twelfth century under Gelasius II (1118–1119) and Calixtus II (1119–1124) the church was modernized

Noteworthy nearby churches

5 **San Giorgio in Velabro**
9 **San Nicola in Carcere**

Santa Maria in Cosmedin

79 Santa Maria in Cosmedin (c. 600, c. 772–795, ninth century and c. 1120). Cross-section showing the *loggia*, temple and, bottom left, crypt. This drawing shows how the shafts of the columns in the crypt have been dug down into the foundations below floor level.

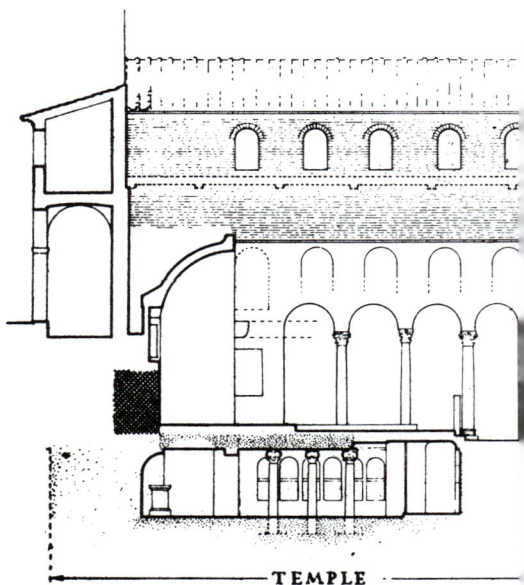

TEMPLE

and rebuilt. Its present appearance is possibly mainly the result of the extensive restoration work carried out in the 1890s by G. B. Giovenale, who returned the church to its 'original' state by stripping away all post-medieval additions. During this restoration work some columns were moved around or replaced altogether.

Exterior

The façade of this relatively small brick-built church was modernized in the early eighteenth century, but the late Baroque ornamentation was removed as part of Giovenale's restoration. Today, with its brick arcades and a porch featuring two sets of spolia columns, the church looks as it would have done in the early twelfth century (pp. 162–163). The two columns at the front of the porch have red granite shafts and fine Ionic capitals (thirteenth century) made especially for this purpose, the two at the back have *fluted pavonazzetto* shafts and modern reconstructions of Ionic capitals. From the portico, where the 'Bocca della verità' has been housed since 1632, three doors lead into the church. The middle door is beautifully framed by ancient ornamented marble posts and lintel, decorated

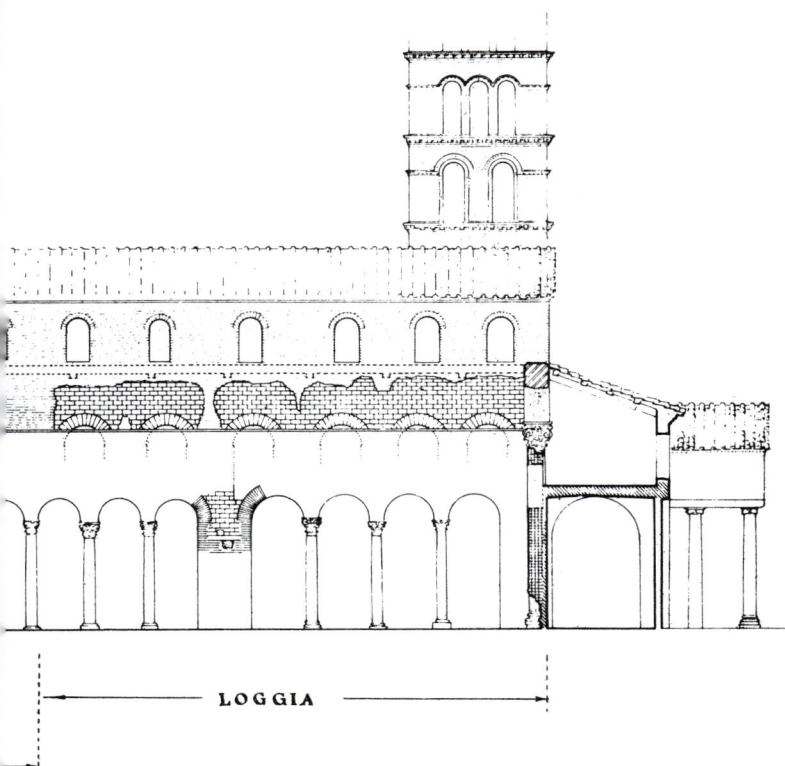

7

Santa Maria in Cosmedin

LOGGIA

on the inside edge with medieval scrolls and animal carvings, probably from the twelfth century and signed by an artist called John of Venice: "IOHANNES DE VENETIA ME FECIT" says the inscription. The doors on either side are framed by narrower marble posts carved with reliefs.

To the right of the church is a lovely twelfth-century *campanile*.

Interior

In size and shape the church now stands as it did after its rebuilding by Pope Adrian I (772–795). But in the entrance wall and on the north side of the nave one can still see some monumental fluted, white marble Composite columns (c. 200) which were part of the loggia (fourth century) into which the church was first incorporated around the year 600 [81]. The original church had the form of a small hall, but in the eight century when it was extended it was furnished with colonnades, which are thought to have supported a trabeation. The church was rebuilt in the ninth century and again

81 Columns in the entrance wall of Santa Maria in Cosmedin, from the original colonnaded *loggia* (fourth century) within which the church was constructed in the sixth century.

82 Detail of the nave, showing the widely differing styles of shafts and capitals in the first three columns on the right-hand side.

in the twelfth century, at which time the trabeation was replaced by arcades and the nave was separated – on both sides – from the side-aisles by three sets of three columns separated by piers [**80**]. These columns vary greatly in terms of type of stone, colour and finish (both smooth and fluted columns), in the style of capital and their ages (figural capitals, Corinthian and Composite in a wide range of styles: dating from antiquity, from fifth-century Byzantium and from the twelfth century) and in the combinations of capitals and

shafts which, as their dimensions reveal, did not originally go together [82] [84]. But during the nineteenth-century restoration,
certain architectural elements were relocated and columns that had
not previously been part of the church were added to the two bays
on either side of *apse*. This makes it difficult to deduce anything
about the arrangement of columns and capitals prior to this, nor
about how the church looked in the eighth or the eleventh century.
Although the church was rebuilt in the twelfth century it seems
likely that some of the columns and capitals from the eighth-
century church were reused then.

In the left side-aisle the sixth column from the entrance presents
a good example of a roughly hewn, inverted Ionic capital used as a
base [83]. Note also the inscribed spolia marble tiles in the floor – as
here, next to this base.

83 Recut, inverted Ionic capital used as a base, sixth column on the left-hand side.
Note the inscribed tile to the left of the base.

84 Santa Maria in Cosmedin. The centre section on the left-hand side, showing three columns with very different shafts and capitals which clearly did not originally go together.

At the centre of the nave is the *schola cantorum*, an enclosed area reserved for the clergy, surrounded by marble panels (from the nineteenth-century restoration) and with a *pergola* or rood-screen separating the *presbytery* from the rest of the church. The *ciborium* is from the end of the thirteenth century. High up on the *clerestory wall*, around the windows, and on the three sides of the apse are the (restored) remains of frescoes which adorned the church in the eighth, ninth and twelfth centuries. The paintings in the colonnade arches date from the nineteenth-century. The church has an exceptionally beautiful *Cosmatesque* floor (from the 1120s), a central feature of which is a huge *rota* of the finest imperial *porphyry* [80].

The crypt

As part of Pope Adrian I's (772–795) extension of the church a crypt was dug out of the ancient Roman *tufa* foundations under the nave (probably the podium of the Ara Maxima Hercules). This small chamber is shaped like a miniature basilica with a nave and two side-aisles, each bounded by three columns (two of pale limestone and four of granite) with Composite, full-leaf, *travertine* capitals (possibly from the latter half of the fourth century or the beginning of the fifth century, though one column is probably a more recent reproduction). The capitals vary in style and, with one possible

85 The crypt under Santa Maria in Cosmedin. Only two of the three columns on each side are visible here.

86 Cross carved into the shaft of one of the columns in the crypt.

exception, did not originally go with these shafts [85]. As can be seen from the cross-section [79] the spolia shafts were a little too tall for the chamber and had to be dug down into the ground a couple of feet. It has been suggested that these columns may have come from the first little church from around the year 600. The different crosses carved into the column shafts show where crosses in a different material (bronze?) once hung – perhaps as a way of Christianizing the 'pagan' stones [86].

Santa Maria in Trastevere

(c. 1140–1148)

Piazza di Santa Maria in Trastevere

7.30 a.m.–9.00 p.m.

SANTA MARIA IN TRASTEVERE's history can be traced back to the founding of the very first Early Christian churches. It is said to be one of the oldest churches in Rome and was also one of the first to be consecrated to the Virgin Mary. The building we see today is, however, the new church built on the foundations of the old by Pope Innocence II around 1140. It is one of the most beautiful churches in the city due to its splendid spolia columns and capitals, its proportions and its mosaics. The magnificent *apse* mosaic dates from the church's construction (c. 1140), the smaller mosaic panels between the windows are by Pietro Cavallini (1291).

Exterior

This lovely brick-built church, with its façade adorned with thirteenth- and fourteenth-century mosaics and its twelfth-century *campanile* was modernized in 1702. This modernization included the addition of a new *portico*, supported by grey granite columns with Ionic capitals made especially for it at this time. Embedded in the walls of the portico, quite densely-packed, are fragments of ancient and medieval inscriptions, gravestones, marble slabs etc. – a practice seen all over Rome (see pp. 174–175) and one which served as a way of preserving and displaying ancient remains [27] [29]. The three doorways, whose positions on the façade were shifted in the sixteenth century, are framed with marble posts dating from Imperial Rome which previously graced the doorways of the twelfth-century church.

Interior

This triple-naved basilica was thoroughly restored in the latter half of the 1860s (by Virginio Vespignani) at which time the floor was lowered to its original level and laid with replicas of the twelfth-thirteenth century *Cosmatesque* flooring, and a new *ciborium* was constructed, using some elements (the four *porphyry* columns and the entablature) from the original twelfth-century ciborium. The church's wooden ceiling is from around 1616 (Domenichino) and the building has been embellished with chapels, tombs and paintings from the sixteenth to the eighteenth centuries. But the splendid

8

Santa Maria in Trastevere

Noteworthy nearby churches

- 2 San Bartolomeo all'Isola
- 3 San Benedetto in Piscinula
- 6 San Crisogono

87 Spolia columns and entablature in Santa Maria in Trastevere. Unlike the rest of the large, matching Ionic capitals in the nave, the last three pairs of columns before the *triumphal arch* sport a variety of Corinthian and (smaller) Ionic capitals.

spolia columns in the colonnades remain unchanged [**87**] [**88**]. There are eleven columns on each side, trabeated as was common with twelfth-century Ionic colonnades. The cornice is supported by *corbels* cut from other marble cornices [**87**].

The *triumphal arch* rests on two columns of grey granite with Corinthian capitals which, in turn, support an exquisite antique entablature.

The shafts of the columns in the nave are of granite, mostly grey (both matte and polished), but also including two pairs in red granite. The wide diversity in the heights and diameters of the shafts has resulted in a motley collection of bases and *plinths* being used to even out the differences in height. Some of the bases are of ancient origin, others are new – which is to say, from the restoration in the 1860s; the plinths are also, for the most part, of modern date [**90**]. The shafts have, to some extent, been arranged in matching pairs lining the central axis, a principle also followed in the ancient capitals which, in the case of the first eight columns, are Ionic. The last three pairs of columns before the triumphal arch are more varied in nature: first a set of red granite shafts (as opposed to the more

89 Ionic capitals from the Baths of Caracalla. The cornice above the beautiful entablature running across the columns is underpinned by small *corbels* carved from different ornamented pieces of other cornices.

predominant grey) with simple Corinthian capitals, then a set of matte-grey granite shafts with simple Ionic capitals and lastly, a pair of granite shafts with grander Corinthian capitals [87]. Where the matte shafts in the colonnades are mainly positioned closest to the apse, those in the first half of the nave have beautifully polished shafts. So, generally speaking, at the top of the nave one finds a combination of polished shafts and relatively large Ionic capitals, while the columns in the colonnades closest to the triumphal arch have matte shafts and a variety of relatively plain capitals. This division of the column elements seems to fit with the differentiation in other churches between the section for laymen, closest to the entrance, and the area closest to the triumphal arch, reserved for the clergy.

After the first two pairs of relatively plain Ionic capitals in the nave come a number of large, exquisitely ornamented Ionic capitals [89]. It has been established that these capitals come from two library arcades in the Baths of Caracalla (c. 220s). These pieces of spolia represent one of the rare cases in which it has proved possible to trace elements back to a specific source. The capitals are adorned with small faces, set in the middle of the square slab at the very top of the capital (the abacus). These are primarily depictions of Serapis and Isis and, in the centre of the volutes, Harpocrates – all characters associated with the Egyptian cult of Isis. Several of the heads were partially hacked away during the restoration in the

90 The right side-aisle of Santa Maria in Trastevere. Some of the columns are set on ornamental bases, which in turn stand on *plinths* of varying heights to compensate for the differing column lengths.

1860s (by anti-idolatry stonemasons). The shafts are of different sorts of granite and a variety of sizes and not all corresponded originally with the capitals they were set to carry in this church. Generally speaking, the capitals here were made for shafts of a greater diameter. As for the bases, four of the ornamented versions may well have come from the Baths of Caracalla.

However, the fact that these spolia came from the thermae still does not explain the ideological motives behind their reuse in this church in the twelfth century. We cannot assume that anyone at that time knew what the building had originally been used for or who the faces were supposed to represent. But these were exceptionally beautiful architectural elements from a monumental ruin which was occasionally referred to, at that time, as a 'palace' from Ancient Rome. So the builders appropriated pieces which quite clearly dated from the Roman Empire. This does not necessarily mean, though, that these elements were chosen as being particularly appropriate for a church dedicated to the Virgin Mary – even if the Harpocrates face, with a hushing finger held to the lips, might seem fitting for a place designed for prayer. And the pairing of capitals featuring a male figure (Serapis) and a female (Isis) was very apt for a church containing an apse mosaic in which Christ and the Virgin sit enthroned. In the twelfth century the faces on the capitals may have been taken to be portraits of a Roman emperor and empress, since it was still known at the time when the church was built that these pieces had come from an Imperial Roman building. Or they may have been reconstrued as Adam and Eve, forerunners to the two figures in the apse mosaic. If that were in fact the case then this could be seen as yet another very typical juxtaposition of old and new; the ancient world (the Roman Empire, the pagan cult and possibly the Old Testament) being replaced by something newer and better (see p. 75).

In addition to using elements from the Baths of Caracalla in this church, Pope Innocence II ordered the building of the splendid arcade in the church of Santo Stefano Rotondo, to provide support for the lofty *clerestory*, which was in danger of collapsing ⑪ [104]. The two granite columns used there are of such massive dimensions that they too could quite conceivably have been appropriated from some ancient thermae. It was, moreover, in the 1140s – during Innocence II's reign – that the French Abbot Suger considered importing columns from the Baths of Diocletian for his rebuilding of the Abbey of Saint Denis near Paris (see pp. 65–66).

San Nicola in Carcere

(Late eleventh century, reconsecrated 1128)
Via del Teatro Marcello 35
7.00 a.m.–5.00 p.m.
Guided tours of the foundations
of the Ancient Roman temple
underneath 10.00 a.m.–5.00 p.m.
(closed Wednesdays).
Enquire in the church.

SAN NICOLA IN CARCERE lies on the site of an old prison – hence the epithet 'in carcere' (in prison). And Saint Nicholas is the patron saint of prisoners. The church is known to have existed since the late eleventh century, but may in fact date from much earlier. It was reconsecrated in 1128, which suggests that significant renovations may have been carried out at this time.

The church incorporates the remains of three Roman temples, to Spes, Juno and Janus, which lay alongside one another in the ancient city's fruit and vegetable market, the Forum Holitorium. The foundations of the middle temple provided the fundament for the church and three columns from its front have been used on the church's façade (pp. 184–185). A row of columns from each of the flanking temples has been built into either side of the church [91]. In Early Christian times and in the Early Middle Ages there had been a reluctance to reusing ancient temples in the construction of churches. This practice was to become more common in the Middle Ages, however – partly because Christianity had become so well-established that there was less need to shun the ancient pagan religion and its buildings, and partly because population levels were so low during this period that smaller churches became more the order of the day. With their small *cella*s ancient temples were suitable for this purpose. In San Nicola in Carcere the inclusion in the building of the three temples did, however, give a much larger interior than would have been the case if only one temple had been converted into a church.

In its present form, with the ancient colonnades on its outer walls now exposed, the church is a typical manifestation of the desire in the Mussolini era (first half of the 1930s) to stress the importance of Ancient Rome at the cost of the Christian Middle Ages. With its demonstration of this early twentieth-century restoration ideal, with its late Renaissance façade, its ornamentation and an interior that was renovated in the fifteenth century and in the seventeenth-eighteenth centuries, and modernized in the nine-

9

San Nicola in Carcere

Noteworthy nearby churches

- **2** San Bartolomeo all'Isola
- **3** San Benedetto in Piscinula
- **5** **San Giorgio in Velabro**
- **13** Santa Maria in Aracoeli [**10**]
- **7** **Santa Maria in Cosmedin**

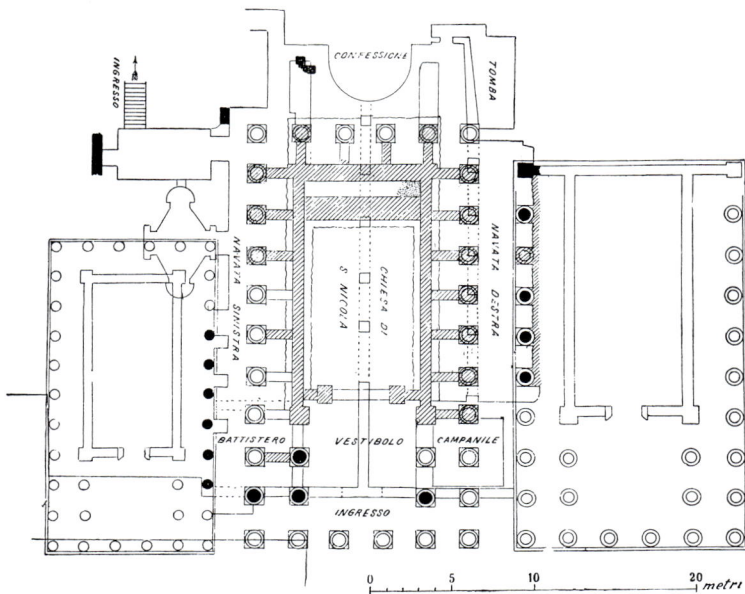

91 Floorplan showing the three temples on which San Nicola in Carcere is in part founded.

teenth century (by Gaspare Servi among others) (*ciborium*, coffered ceiling, wall and apse frescoes) San Nicola in Carcere presents an excellent illustration of the gradual build-up of historical layers in the buildings of Rome.

Exterior

On the church's north side the restoration conducted during the Mussolini era exposed the Ionic *peperino* colonnade and entablature from the Temple of Janus (third century BC) (pp. 184–185), while the south side is graced with *travertine* Doric columns and entablature from the Temple of Spes (third century BC). Giacomo Della Porta's façade from 1599 incorporates two stuccoed columns from the middle Temple of Juno and a third (in peperino) was exposed on the façade during the restoration in the 1930s.

Interior

Inside the triple-naved basilica one is also reminded of the building's ancient foundations by a slight indent in the walls on either side of the central nave just before the last two pairs of columns [**92**]. The church features a wonderful variety of columns (not including the bases, which were replaced during the nineteenth-century restoration of the church): the two rows of seven columns

92 San Nicola in Carcere,
looking towards the apse (around 1100).

93 Floorplan of San Nicola in Carcere.

Grey granite

Grey granite

Cipollino

Cipollino — Portasanta

Cipollino — Cipollino

Red granite — Cipollino

Grey marble — Cipollino

Granite

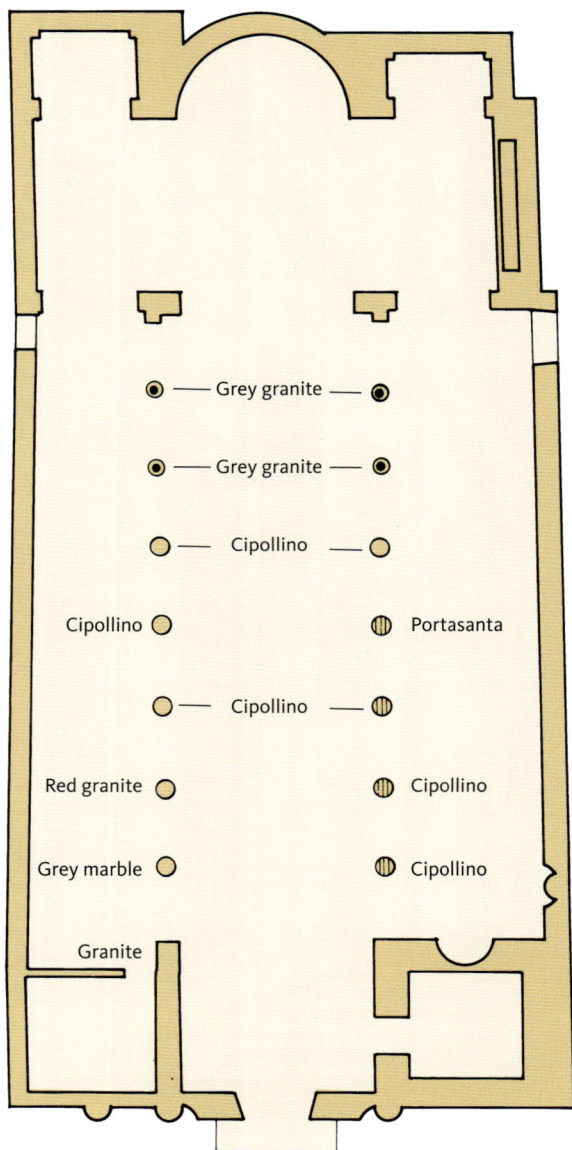

Ionic, smooth shaft
Corinthian, smooth shaft
Corinthian, fluted shaft

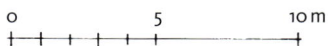

0 — 5 — 10 m

San Nicola in Carcere

9

94 The two Ionic columns closest to the *triumphal arch*, right-hand side.

running down the nave contrast with, rather than mirror each other, as was the more common practice. Only the last two pairs of columns before the chancel adhere to this mirroring principle [**93**]. On the right-hand side the first three columns are of *fluted*, green-streaked *cipollino*, the fourth – also fluted – is of red *portasanta* and the fifth has a smooth cipollino shaft. All have Corinthian capitals (mid-third century). The last two columns before the chancel have grey granite shafts and Ionic capitals, the first of these being small and plain, the second larger and slightly more elaborate [**94**]. The first five columns on the left-hand side are rather more uniform in appearance. Here, too, though, the type of stone varies: the first shaft is of grey marble, the next is red granite (a nineteenth-cent-ury addition with a capital from Asia Minor) and the following three are of green-streaked cipollino. All of the capitals on these columns are Corinthian (first-second centuries). The last two columns before the chancel are of grey granite with Ionic capitals (the sixth possibly third-century, the seventh possibly early second century) like their opposite numbers on the right side. So, while there is no correspondence between the first four sets of columns, the fifth pair do match (both having smooth cipollino shafts) and these are followed by the two pairs of identical grey-granite Ionic columns.

This arrangement of the different elements could be interpreted as a way of creating a demarcation and a certain hierarchy within the nave: at the end nearest the entrance there is a differentiation between the right and the left sides, with the most finely wrought and varied materials on the right side fitting with the higher status accorded to this (the male) side of the church, as was probably also the case in San Giorgio in Velabro ❺ (p. 142). At the far end of the nave, closest to the *triumphal arch*, the matching pairs of columns define the area which was in all probability reserved for the clergy. The culmination of the colonnade in the modest, granite Ionic columns may have been conceived as an illustration, or concrete expression, of the Christian ideals of simplicity and asceticism as befitting the members of the church, as in San Giorgio in Velabro (pp. 142–145).

Another distinctive feature of the church's right side is the second column in the colonnade which bears an inscription possibly dating from the seventh-eighth centuries [**95**]. This inscription reads "Anastasius, maiordomus [a senior church official], gives gifts to Saint Anna, Simeon and [the Church of Saint] Lucia". This tells us that this column has previously been part of an older church, to which it was donated by the aforementioned Anastasius. Another inscription just above the base of the column states that someone (probably Anastasius) is buried under this column – or at least, where this column originally stood before it was moved, as spolia, for the second time to its present location in San Nicola. Near the column, on the wall of the nave, a third inscription details the gifts made to the church by a twelfth-century priest, Romanus (probably under Pope Urban II, 1088–1099). This inscription and Romanus's donations seem almost to echo the actions of his predecessor, Anastasius, just as the column provides an echo, here, of its function in an earlier church. This column has evidently been viewed as a relic of sorts from an older and hence highly regarded church. Its inclusion in San Nicola endowed the new building with some of the authority and prestige of the original church.

95 San Nicola in Carcere: column (second on left-hand side) bearing an inscription which testifies to the column's earlier use in another church.

✝ D E D O N I S D I E T
SCE DI GENETRICI MARIE
SCE ANNE SCS SIMEONETS
LUCIE EQ O ANASTASIUS
IO A DOMU OFERO RO BIS PRO
ICIES BES TRE BINEA TAB
✝ IN PORTU SEU
BO BES PARIA IUMENTAS
XXX PORCI X FUR MADERAE
XX VECTUS IT RATU NU
TE PBR SE VALEO LECTOS
IO AT MANSIONARIIS
SEQUEN TIBUS

✝ IC REQUIESCIT

Santa Sabina (c. AD 422–432)

Piazza Pietro d'Illiria
Open: 08.15 a.m.–12.30 p.m. +
3.30 p.m.–6.00 p.m.

SANTA SABINA sits on the peaceful, leafy Aventine Hill, next to an orange grove and with a magnificent view of the city and St Peter's. The church was restored in 1914–1919 by Antonio Muñoz and again in the latter half of the 1930s. During these restorations various alterations and additions made in the late fifteenth and the sixteenth centuries were stripped away and the Medieval furnishings and ornamentation reconstructed so that this beautiful church now looks more or less as it did when it was built. It is, therefore, a rare and perfect example in style and form of the Early Christian basilica. A mosaic inscription on the wall of the vestibule or *narthex* tells us that the church was founded by the presbyter Peter of Illyria [**100**]. It was built during the reign of Pope Celestine I (422–432) and was possibly completed under Sixtus III (432–440). The basilica was built on top of and incorporates some of the stonework and foundations of the old Roman buildings which previously occupied this site. Today the underlying structure can be discerned in the exposed column rising up out of the floor of the church against the wall of the right-hand side-aisle [**96**] and in the grille-covered opening in the paving of the narthex, offering a glimpse of a marble floor beneath. A staircase at the top of the right-hand side-aisle leads down to a series of rooms (third century) beneath the church; viewing by appointment. Also by appointment it is possible to visit the fine thirteenth-century cloister which is reached from the narthex.

The exterior

Outwardly the church is a typical example of the Early Christian basilica: a simple, unadorned brick building with a run of tall windows dominating the *clerestory* wall and the semi-circular *apse* of the church, giving some idea of what an important part light played as a metaphor for divinity (pp. 194–195). The modest restraint of the exterior is counterbalanced, however, by the richness of the materials and ornamentation of the interior.

Across the west front of the church runs a *narthex*, with entrance from just the one side. The narthex was reconstructed during the twentieth-century restoration of the church using spolia unearthed

Noteworthy nearby churches

24 Santa Prisca
27 San Saba

96 Column from the Roman house under Santa Sabina, now exposed in the wall on the right-hand side of the church.

during excavations conducted in the course of the rebuilding: four *spiral-fluted* marble columns along one wall of the narthex and four granite columns on the opposite wall, all without capitals. In the west front are two very different spolia doorways dating from the time when the church was built (the third, leading to the left-hand side-aisle was walled-up during the building of the *campanile*). Of these two doorways, the left (the central entrance), features a direct transposition to the church of a temple doorway: a beautifully pro-filed and ornamented marble door-frame [**97**]. The doors them-selves are decorated with remarkable wood-carvings dating back to the fifth century (containing the first ever depictions in Early Christ-ian Art of the Crucifixion). In these carvings, events from the Old Testament are paired with events from the New, a common artistic ploy of the period. Generally speaking, it is a way of contrasting the old and the new; the old acquiring fresh value by being set against the new – which also ties in with the principle behind the use of spolia (see p. 75). Unlike the straightforward reuse of the frame from the temple portal, the right-hand doorway exemplifies a more inventive use of spolia [**98**]. In this case the *lintel* is a *soffit*, which is

97 The central doorway on the west side of Santa Sabina, taken from the entrance to the *cella* (inner chamber) of an ancient temple. The wooden doors carved with reliefs are the original ones from the church's construction in the fifth century.

to say the underside of the marble *architrave* which, in classic architecture, rests on the columns. In its new function this trabeation has, however, been turned ninety degrees so that its bottom faces outwards. Thus the relief work, the curved contours of which mark its original setting on the two circular capitals, is now a purely decorative motif. The door is crowned by a section of an antique cornice. The church's two doorways testify to the fact that the builders were quite capable of placing a one-to-one transposition and a radically original, recycled composition side by side.

On the south side of the church, facing onto the square in front of the building is a more recent entrance from the fifteenth century with a Corinthian *portico* in which the two centre *travertine*-faced columns are topped by antique Corinthian capitals.

The interior

The church, a triple-naved basilica, is unusual in that it is constructed around a set of identical columns complete with capitals. The two rows of twelve, partially *fluted* columns are of *Proconnesian* marble and have Corinthian capitals and bases (late third century) [**99**]. The materials probably came from a depot of building materials; they may have become available due to the sacking of Rome by Alaric and the Visigoths in AD 410, the first of a series of assaults on the once mighty city by tribes from the north. Buildings were wrecked and burned, but the remains could then be brought back into play – in the building of a new church, for example. Tradition has it that the columns stem from the ruined Temple of Juno Regina on the Aventine Hill, and the Corinthian order would certainly be apt, both for this mother goddess and for a female Christian saint. But there does not seem to be any hard evidence to support this theory, and partially fluted columns were not normally used in temples.

98 Doorway in the west-facing entrance wall with the entrance to Santa Sabina's right-hand side-aisle. The door is framed by two marble entablatures while a *soffit*, i.e. the underside of a marble trabeation originally supported by two columns, has been turned 90 degrees and used as a lintel. The doorway is topped by a hefty cornice.

Santa Sabina

99 Santa Sabina, looking towards the apse (c. 422–432). The basilica has three naves separated by two rows of twelve identical *half-fluted* marble columns with Corinthian capitals from the late second century. The marble revetment in the apse is a modern reconstruction in grey-veined marble and *porphyry*.

100 Fifth-century mosaic on the entrance wall of Santa Sabina.

CAELESTINVSHABERET
ETEPISCOPVSORBE
AVITPRESBYTERVRBIS
SVIRNOMINETANTO
INVTRITVSINAVLA
AVPERQVIBONAVITAE
VITSPERAREFVTVRAM

ECLESIAEX
CENTIVS

The later church of Santo Stefano Rotondo (the 460s AD) contains, as it happens, another four Corinthian capitals which are believed to come from the same series as those at Santa Sabina ⓫ [108].

In Rome only the slightly later San Pietro in Vincoli [15] and to some extent Santa Maria Maggiore [16] can boast as uniform a selection of spolia as that found at Santa Sabina, which suggests either that it was very rare for builders to have a whole building to draw on for a new church or – more probably – that they simply preferred combinations of different elements. Even in the 'classical', uniform Santa Sabina only selected elements from an ancient building have been used: the entablature which the columns would have supported in the original, antique building has been rejected in favour of a non-classical combination of columns and arcades. As with the church's *soffit*-crowned doorway [98], in which antique materials have been used in new ways, a kind of Early Christian counterpoint to the uniform design of the columns has been created. The incorporation of the old architectural elements in the new arcade construction (see p. 34) results in a subtle break with the tradition inherent in these ancient columns, with their potential classical, pagan associations. The materials and the fine workmanship of the antique columns were evidently appreciated and admired – but only if set into a new context.

That the church should have two rows of twelve columns is hardly a coincidence. The widespread interest in the symbolism of numbers made this particular number especially appropriate for a church, as a symbol of the twelve apostles, the pillars of the church (see p. 59). Here, too, the way in which the antique elements have been used points to a reinterpretation of the columns – or the attribution to them of a significance that transcends their ancient origins.

The church's *schola cantorum* was reconstructed during the restoration in the 1930s, using marble panels from a similar structure from the ninth century.

Originally, the walls under the windows in the light-filled central nave were covered with mosaics, but no traces of these survive. Only in the *narthex* does one beautiful mosaic still remain. On this an inscription in gold on a blue ground describes the church's founding [100]. The space above the arcades and the walls of the semi-circular apse are decorated with typical Early Christian panels in *opus sectile* (fifth-sixth century, reconstructed during the twentieth-century restoration) – thin slices of different sorts of marble and *porphyry* laid in patterns with a stylized chalice as a recurring

101 Detail of columns and Corinthian capitals supporting an arcade decorated with marble *opus sectile*.

motif [**101**]. The mosaics which originally adorned the *triumphal arch* (depicting the sacred cities of Bethlehem and Jerusalem) and the vault of the apse are echoed in the sixteenth century frescoes (by Taddeo Zuccari, restored in the 1830s). So the overall look of the church interior was much more colourful and full of reflected light from the mosaics than it is today.

Note the exquisite latticework of the windows (modern reconstructions). These are fitted with finely ground, transparent panes of *selenite* (gypsum crystal) which was used in the Middle Ages instead of glass; proper glass did not become widely used in ecclesiastical architecture until the advent of the Gothic period in the thirteenth century.

Santo Stefano Rotondo

(c. 460s)

Via di Santo Stefano Rotondo 6

9.30 a.m.–12.30 p.m. + Winter: 2.00 p.m.–5.00 p.m. /
Summer: 3.00 p.m.–6.00 p.m.
(closed Monday and Sunday afternoons).
The mithraeum is seldom
open to visitors.

THE SANTO STEFANO ROTONDO of today is a somewhat reduced version of the original church, which was rebuilt during the Renaissance. But with its vast, circular chambers it is nonetheless a quite unique building as far as Rome is concerned. The church was probably founded in the early 460s and was consecrated during the reign of Pope Simplicius (468–483). It was erected (with imperial permission) on the site of an old barracks and, like San Clemente ❸ [53], over a *mithraeum* (second century) which, in Santo Stefano is adorned with well-preserved frescoes (third century).

Exterior

In its original form the simple concentric, red-brick central building from the latter half of the fifth century seems to have been symmetrical in layout with no one main entrance. Under Pope Innocence II (1130–1143) it was furnished with a *portico* supported by four grey granite columns topped, not by capitals, but by white marble *imposts* (pp. 206–207).

By the fifteenth century Santo Stefano was in serious danger of collapsing and Pope Nicholas V (1447–1455) commissioned architect Bernardo Rossellino (possibly assisted by the famous scholar and architect Leon Battista Alberti) to carry out restoration work on the church. This entailed tearing down the greater part of the outer, and apparently most dilapidated, ring of the building [102] [105].

Interior

The layout of the original, larger church was complex [102]. In its overall design it was a circular building with three concentric *ambulatories* surrounding a tall, drum-shaped central chamber. Onto this circular structure was superimposed the shape of a cross with each of the four arms ending in a large *narthex*-style chamber.

Noteworthy nearby churches

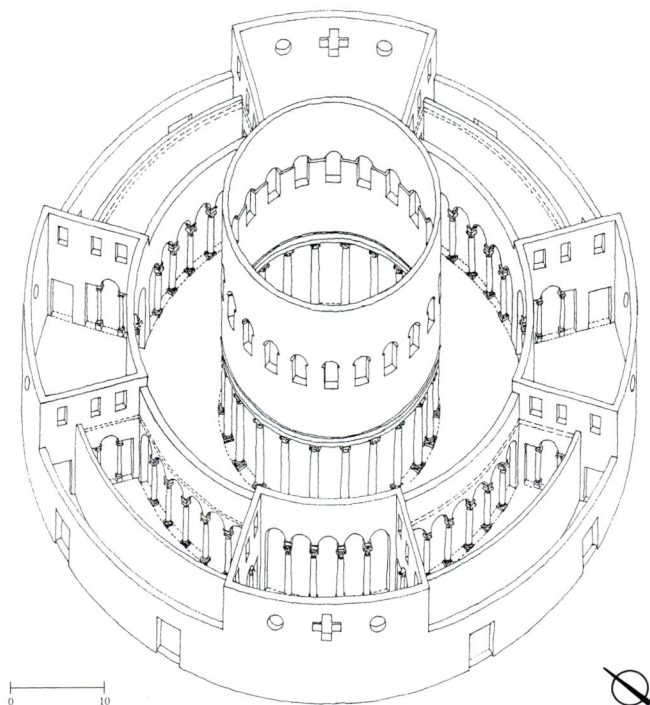

102 Santo Stefano Rotondo. Reconstruction of the original floorplan (according to Hugo Brandenburg).

The church could be entered through the *ambulatories* in the outer rings, which gave onto the four narthexes, and from these one could pass into the middle ambulatory or go straight into the ambulatory around the central chamber. Today the church is entered via the ambulatory to the right of the north-eastern narthex [**103**].

By the twelfth century, during the reign of Pope Innocence II (1130–1143), the tall drum-shaped wall of the central chamber was dangerously close to collapsing. It was therefore reinforced by the addition of an arcade consisting of three transverse arches supported in the centre by two colossal Corinthian columns in grey granite and at either end by a pier topped by a square Corinthian capital of grey-streaked (*Proconnesian?*) marble [**107**]. The cylindrical wall was further strengthened by the bricking up of fourteen of the *clerestory*'s twenty-two windows [**104**].

The columns used in the construction of the church are a combination of spolia and Late Antique elements, probably from one of the depots of serially produced pieces which still to be found in the fifth century.

103 Santo Stefano Rotondo viewed from the north-eastern *narthex* (c. 460s).

104 Arcade supported by two huge spolia columns with grey granite shafts and Corinthian capitals. The arcade was built during the reign of Pope Innocence II (1130–1143) to reinforce the high walls of the central chamber which were in danger of collapsing.

The central chamber is bounded by a circle of twenty-two granite Ionic columns supporting a necessarily curving entablature of Proconnesian marble designed specifically for this building [**103**]. The Ionic capitals are of Roman make, probably from the late fourth or early fifth century. Minor differences in the size and style of the various elements suggest that these were stock items rather than pieces designed specially for the church. Certain spolia have been used specifically to highlight one axis – that formed by one arm of the implicit cross in the plan of the church – as the most important: the north-eastern narthex is separated from the central ambulatory by four spolia columns with grey-granite shafts and Corinthian full-leaf capitals (late second century) [**106**]. Opposite these, on the wall facing what was once the south-western narthex, are spolia columns with *fluted* marble shafts and Corinthian capitals (late second century) [**108**]. These capitals are thought to belong to the same series as those in Santa Sabina **10** [**99**] and must have lain unused for decades after the first twenty-four were used in the other church. These columns have ordinary fluted shafts as opposed to Santa Sabina's *half-fluted* versions. The transverse arm of the cross (where,

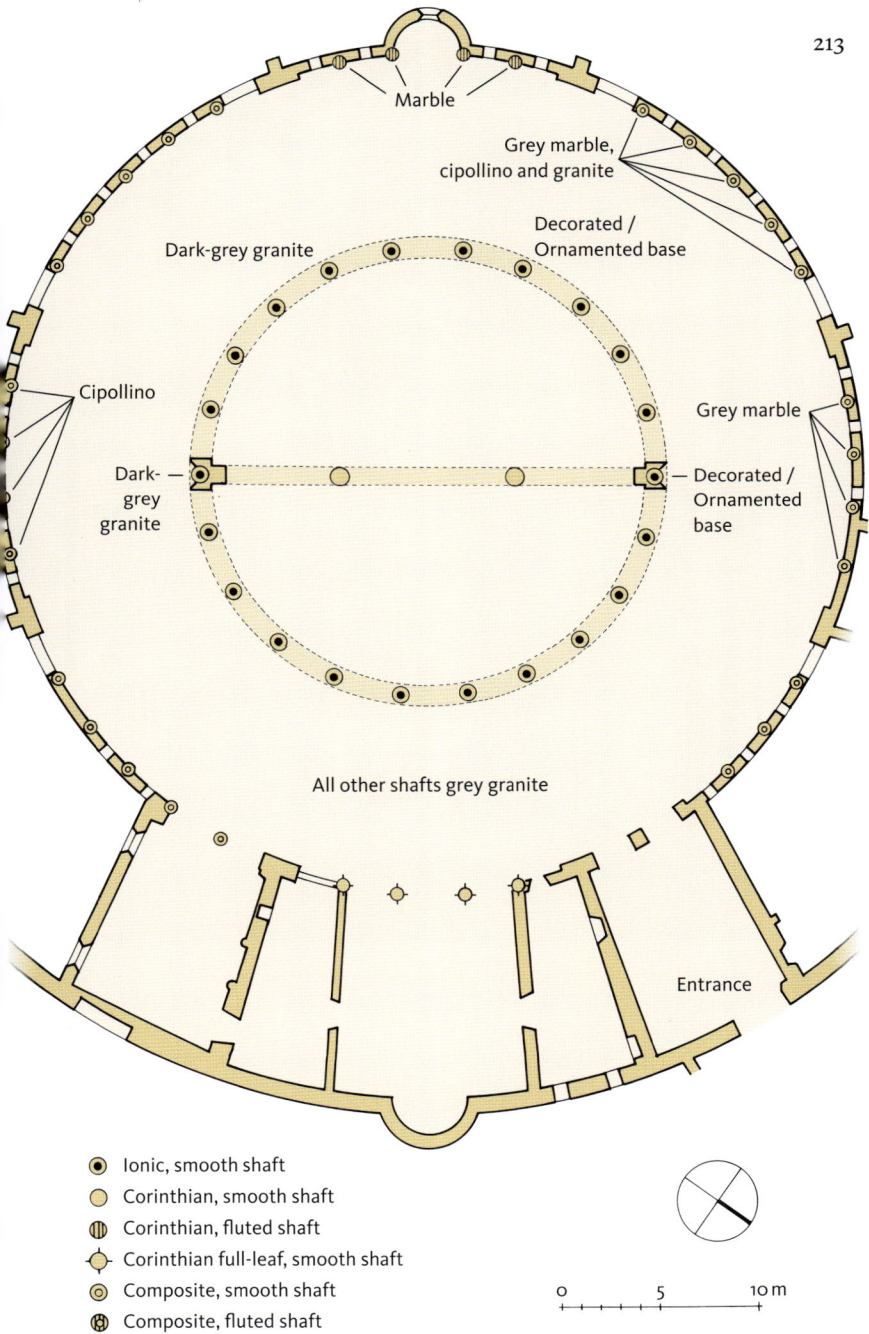

Marble

Grey marble,
cipollino and granite

Decorated /
Ornamented base

Dark-grey granite

Cipollino

Grey marble

Dark-
grey
granite

Decorated /
Ornamented
base

All other shafts grey granite

Entrance

⊙ Ionic, smooth shaft
◯ Corinthian, smooth shaft
▥ Corinthian, fluted shaft
✦ Corinthian full-leaf, smooth shaft
◎ Composite, smooth shaft
✪ Composite, fluted shaft

o   5   10 m

105 Floorplan of Santo Stefano Rotondo as it has looked since the
demolition of the outer ring of chambers in the fifteenth century.

106 Santo Stefano Rotondo: four spolia columns with granite shafts and Corinthian full-leaf capitals (late third century) separating the *ambulatory* from what was originally the north-eastern *narthex*.

originally, there would have been two additional narthexes) is defined by minor variations in the fabric of the columns. Where the circle of columns is crowned by an entablature the other columns support arcades. This is true both of the massive spolia columns in the two narthexes on the church's central axis and the smaller columns separating the central ambulatory from the outer one (most of which was torn down in the fifteenth century) [**109**]. The smaller columns in the outer circle are of different sorts of stone (*cipollino*, grey marble and granite) with Ionic capitals, also from the late fourth or early fifth century [**105**]. In the south-eastern arm

107 The outer piers of the arcade partially enclose the columns on the church's central axis. These columns are also of a slightly darker granite than the others. In addition, the one on the north side, seen here, stands on a distinctive ornamented base. The floor was being repaired when this picture was taken.

108 Four spolia columns with *fluted* marble shafts and Corinthian capitals (late third century). The columns are set into the outer wall of the church, but they originally separated the *ambulatory* from the south-western *narthex* which was removed in the fifteenth century when the church was rebuilt in a reduced form. The capitals probably come from the same source as the set of twenty-four in Santa Sabina 🔟 [**101**].

109 Santo Stefano Rotondo's outer circle of columns. Here, marking the eastern arm of the transverse axis, two columns with *fluted cipollino* shafts and Ionic capitals present a contrast to the other, smooth-shafted, Ionic columns in the outer circle. These columns are now set into the wall, but they originally bounded onto the outer *ambulatory*, which was pulled down in the fifteenth century.

Santo Stefano Rotondo

of the cross a couple of fluted cipollino shafts mark the original entrance into the narthex, while the narthex in the north-western arm contains less eye-catching smooth, grey, marble shafts. The variations in stone and style of the columns in the inner circle around the central chamber also seem to have served to define the structure of the church. At either end of the transverse axis stands a column with a dark, grey granite shaft, and the one facing the north-western arm of the cross rests on a distinctive ornamented base [**107**]

[110]. Another of the shafts in the central circle – the first of the four columns marking the entrance to the south-western narthex – stands on a similar ornamented base. The subtle differences in tone of the grey granite shafts are possibly too slight to indicate any conscious plan in their arrangement. Only the general sensibility at that time to the qualities of the different elements and the widespread fondness for using particularly distinctive columns as a means of defining a space gives any reason for assuming (but no proof) that the arrangement and juxtaposition of these pieces in Santa Stefano is not accidental.

The number twenty-two, which occurs in the central circle of columns and in the windows of the clerestory, was interpreted by contemporary theologians as being symbolic of the relationship between the Old and New Testaments and thus it typifies the medieval tendency to regard the things of the old world as imperfect forerunners to those of the new (see pp. 75–76). The practice of using spolia, whereby pieces from the past were employed in a new and better fashion, was in itself an expression of this way of thinking.

110 Base in the inner circle of columns on the north-eastern arm of the transverse axis.

11

Santo Stefano Rotondo

Practical Information

Other noteworthy spolia churches

T HE CHURCHES LISTED HERE are merely a selection of the most interesting as regards the use of spolia. There are, though, countless other churches in Rome which contain at least some, if not many ancient architectural elements.

Dating

In most cases, the dating of the churches is only approximate. Often we only know under which pope a church was consecrated. For this reason the years of the relevant pope's reign are quoted as a guideline for the age of the church. But work could have begun much earlier or perhaps it was reconsecrated due to a or reconstruction. Moreover, the majority of churches contain later additions and have been restored in more recent times. So a building cannot really be attributed to one specific period. Instead it has undergone a centuries-long process of change and alteration, and who is to say that one stage in the construction of a church has greater historical validity than another? In the following list, the dates given denote the time when the church was first erected and when significant later reconstruction or restoration work was carried out.

Visiting the churches

Apart from the four major pilgrim basilicas (St Peter's, San Giovanni in Laterano, Santa Maria Maggiore and San Paolo fuori le Mura) and a few other very well visited churches which remain open all day, churches close for lunch, usually from around 12.30 p.m. to 4.30 or 5.00 p.m. Most churches open early in the morning, around 7.30–8.00, and close around 6.00–7.00 p.m.

Visitors to the churches should respect the dress codes for what is considered acceptable attire: women are asked to make sure their shoulders and upper arms are covered and not wear shorts or very short skirts, men should wear long trousers. Wandering around a church during services is frowned upon, so Sunday is not the best day for sightseeing since mass is held several times during the day.

The taking of photographs is permitted (but not the use of tripods). Some places do not allow flash photography though.

Other noteworthy spolia churches

❶ The Lateran Baptistery, pp. 36, 45, 57–59, **86–99**, 127

The Lateran Basilica: see San Giovanni in Laterano

Pantheon: see Santa Maria Rotonda

❶ Sant'Adriano, p. 52

The Curia Senatus, official seat of the Senate of Rome in the Forum Romanum (rebuilt after a fire in 303) was converted into a church by Pope Honorius I in 630 and restored and remodelled several times during the Middle Ages. It has now been restored to its 'bare' ancient appearance. In 1660 Pope Alexander VII had the church's antique bronze doors moved to San Giovanni in Laterano for use in the main entrance ❼.

❷ Sant'Agnese fuori le Mura (pp. 36–37, 49, **100–111**, 126 [**64**]

❷ San Bartolomeo all'Isola

This church, which sits on Tiber Island, was built at the end of the tenth century by the (German) Holy Roman Emperor, Otto III, probably on the spot where the Temple of Aesculapius lay in ancient times. It was rebuilt by Pope Paschal II (1099–1118) and restored and modernized again in the decades around 1600 and in the nineteenth century. The triple-naved church has seven antique columns running down either side, with shafts, bases and *plinths* of varying sizes. Most of the shafts are of grey or red granite, but there are also three shafts of light and dark marble and the columns are not arranged in matching pairs. The capitals, painted and gilded in the nineteenth century, are Composite. Note also the well-head (c. 1000) carved out of the base drum of an ancient column and decorated with reliefs depicting St Adalbert, St Bartholomew and Otto III framed by different types of column [**9**].

❸ San Benedetto in Piscinula

Probably one of Rome's smallest churches, but no less delightful for that – quite the opposite in fact. The church dates probably from the late eleventh or early twelfth century. A *narthex* gives on to the triple-naved basilica which contains just eight columns in all, featuring a fine variety of spolia elements. *Cosmatesque* floor from the twelfth century.

4 Santa Bibiana

This church constitutes a small Early-Christian enclave right alongside the tracks of Stazione Termini, Rome's main railway station. It dates back to the fifth century, but was restored in the thirteenth century. The eight fine spolia columns in the nave, four on each side, support an entablature. The columns are arranged in matching pairs: the first two have red granite shafts with Corinthian capitals, then come a couple of grey columns and a couple of red with Composite full-leaf capitals and lastly a splendid pair of *half-fluted*, spiral columns of *Proconnesian* marble with beautifully carved Composite capitals. The chapel in the right-hand side-aisle contains another (smaller) pair of column shafts of this same type. The church was restored and remodelled by the famous Baroque architect and sculptor G.L. Bernini around 1625.

3 **San Clemente** pp. 41, 50–51, **112–123**

5 **Santi Cosma e Damiano**, p. 51 [**19**]

The entrance to the church is on the Via dei Fori Imperiali, but its imposing, early spolia doorway overlooks the Forum Romanum. The doorway is part of the audience chamber, often referred to as the Temple of Romulus (post 307), which was converted into the vestibule of the church in the first half of the sixth century. The bronze doors of the audience chamber are also spolia, from around 200. The church's seventeenth-century (and spolia free) interior is particularly notable for the magnificent mosaics in the apse, which date from as far back as the consecration of the church around 530.

4 **Santa Costanza**, pp. 59, 102, **124–135**

6 **San Crisogono**, pp. 50, 59

This church from the first half of the twelfth century features restored granite shafts and seventeenth-century Ionic capitals in the nave, two splendid Corinthian *porphyry* columns (the largest in Rome) in the *triumphal arch* and a beautiful *Cosmatesque* floor. San Crisogno is built on top of an older, columnless church dating back to the early fourth century (with frescoes from the sixth to the tenth centuries) which is open to visitors.

5 **San Giorgio in Velabro,** pp. 37, 79–82, 103, **136–145**, 192

Other noteworthy spolia churches

7 **San Giovanni in Laterano** (the Lateran Basilica), pp. 13, 28–31, 79, 221 [**4**] [**5**]

The cathedral of Rome and one of the seven pilgrim basilicas. Founded by the Emperor Constantine around 313, the year when he issued the Edict of Milan, legalizing Christianity. The Lateran Basilica, which was originally dedicated to Christ the Saviour, is the first church to be officially built in Rome and possibly in the world. The five-naved basilica was restored and rebuilt several times during the Middle Ages with, for example, the original column-borne entablatures in the nave being replaced at one point by arcades. The last major re-build of the church was carried out between 1646 and 1650 by architect Francesco Borromini who encapsulated the old building within a Baroque shell. Borromini did, however, restore and reuse the green marble columns from the colonnades in the Early Christian basilica's side-aisles in the sculpture niches in the nave [**5**]. Around 1600 the large Chapel of the Blessed Sacrament was constructed around some superb ancient gilded bronze columns (from the time of the Emperor Hadrian) which were in all probability a feature of the church in Constantine's day. The bronze doors in the main entrance came from the Curia Senatus (the Senate House), which was converted into the church of Sant'Adriano **1** in the seventh century. The doors were moved to the Lateran Basilica by Pope Alexander VII (1655–1667) in 1660. Do not miss the lovely cloister by Vassalletto with its *Cosmatesque* mosaics (1215–1232).

San Giovanni in Laterano Baptistery/ San Giovanni in Fonte: see **1** the Lateran Baptistery

8 **San Giovanni a Porta Latina** [**26**]

This simple, lovely church is dedicated to St John the Evangelist and lies just inside the city wall by the Porta Latina. The first church was raised on this spot at the end of the fifth century. It was restored by Pope Adrian I (772–795) and rebuilt in 1119 after the devastation caused by the Normans in 1084. The church's *portico* with its four spolia columns (one of *cipollino*, two of granite, one of *fluted* marble) and their capitals – one Tuscan and three Ionic – is from the twelfth century. Inside, the church has two rows of Ionic columns running down the nave: five on either side with shafts of different materials (red and grey granite, cipollino, fluted *pavonazzetto*) arranged in pairs crosswise along the axis of the nave. The column shafts are of different lengths and are therefore set on antique bases of varying heights. All except for the last pair, that is: these two columns have no base, but stand on the floor itself. Of the Ionic capitals, two are of ancient origin, while the rest were made for the church in the twelfth century. Note the remains in the *presbytery* of the exquisite *Cosmatesque* floor complete with many instances of inscriptions. See also the beautiful frescoes from around 1200 depicting scenes from the Old and the New Testaments. During the first half of the twentieth century the Baroque ornamentation was removed from the church when it was restored to the way it might have looked in the Middle Ages. At this same time the floor was also lowered to its original level.

9 **Santi Giovanni e Paolo**, pp. 50, 59

This church, located in a peaceful spot next to a park, the Villa Celimontana, was built around 410 on the site of an older (fourth century) *titulus* constructed within an even older Roman building complete with a *nymphaeum*, some fine, well-preserved wall paintings (third and fourth century), floor mosaics and more (entrance to the *Case romane* in the Clivo Scauro, open to visitors 10.00 a.m.–1.00 p.m. and 3.00 p.m.–6.00 p.m., closed Tues. and Wed.). The *portico* of the church is from the twelfth century (restored in the mid-twentieth century). In the centre of its façade are six Ionic columns of grey and red granite (with twelfth-century capitals), while the outermost columns on either side are of marble with Corinthian full-leaf capitals. High on the façade of the nave is another small arcade supported by four marble Corinthian columns. When the church was last restored (in the twentieth century) two white marble Composite columns from the original *narthex* were exposed on either side of the entrance. The interior of the church was thoroughly modernized during the years 1715–1718, at which time the floor was raised, partially concealing the high *plinths* on which the twelve pairs of granite Corinthian columns in the two colonnades rest, and the massive piers were incorporated into the arcades, thus effectively camouflaging the varied nature of the spolia.

6 **San Lorenzo fuori le Mura**, pp. 30, 40, 59, 71, *77–78*, **146–161**

Other noteworthy spolia churches

⑩ San Lorenzo in Miranda (Temple of Antoninus and Faustina), p. 56 [**21**]

This church is housed in the Ancient Roman Temple of Antoninus and Faustina (c. 140). It is first mentioned in written sources from the late twelfth century, but the building may have been converted to a church as far back as the seventh or eighth centuries. The beautiful Corinthian columns of green-streaked *cipollino* marble from the front of the original temple now support the *portico* gracing the façade from 1602 – at which time the interior of the church was completely reconstructed (without using spolia).

⑪ Santa Maria degli Angeli, p. 52

Constructed within the Baths of Diocletian (c. 300) according to designs by Michelangelo from the early 1560s. Thoroughly modernized by Luigi Vanvitelli in 1749.

⑫ Santa Maria Antiqua, p. 52

(Admission by appointment only)

This church, situated in the Forum Romanum was probably constructed in the 570s within a first-century secular building which may have been a guardroom or a vestibule of the Imperial palace on the Palatine Hill. The building's original piers were replaced by eight grey granite, Corinthian columns, four on either side of the nave. The church walls are decorated with lovely, early medieval frescoes. It fell into disuse in the ninth century, probably after being damaged in a violent earthquake in 847. Another church, Santa Maria Liberatrice, which was built on this site in the early seventeenth century, was demolished around 1900 to allow the excavation of Santa Maria Antiqua.

⑬ Santa Maria in Aracoeli, pp. 59, 66–67, 76 [**10**]

An exceptionally large and beautiful church which stands on the Capitol, right next to the Palazzo Senatorio, the town hall of Rome. Santa Maria in Aracoeli was built in the second half of the thirteenth century on the site of an older church. The nave is lined by forty-four beautifully varied spolia columns, twenty-two on each side (a number regarded in numerology as symbolic of the relationship between the Old and New Testaments see pp. 75–76). The shafts are of red and grey granite and different sorts of marble, both *fluted* and smooth, teamed with a wide range of different capitals and bases. The third column on the left bears the inscription 'ACVBICVLO AVGVSTORVM' (from the bedroom of the Augustuses) [25]. The capital lettering here is possibly a medieval or early Renaissance imitation of an ancient inscription. According to legend (as retold, for example, in Jacopo Voragine's *Legenda Aurea* from c. 1260, i.e. around the time of the church's construction) the church was built after the Emperor Augustus had a vision in which he saw the Virgin with the Christ Child on an altar in heaven. The church's name, Aracoeli, means heavenly altar. The inscription on the column appears to speak of the Emperor Augustus, suggesting this is actually a piece of spolia from his palace.

❼ Santa Maria in Cosmedin, pp. 52, 79–82, **162–173**

⓮ Santa Maria in Domnica, p. 48 [18]
A beautiful church from the first half of the ninth century featuring a relatively uniform collection of spolia in the form of nine pairs of fine Corinthian columns lining the nave. The shafts are of grey granite, all except the first two on the left-hand side which are of red granite. The capitals (first to fifth century plus one from the ninth century) are of Roman and Byzantine origin. Further variation is provided by the two splendid *porphyry* columns supporting the *triumphal arch*. The apse and the wall of the triumphal arch are adorned with magnificent mosaics from the time of Pope Paschal I (817–824).

⓯ Santa Maria Egiziaca (the Temple of Portunus or the Temple of Fortuna Virilis), pp. 53–56
(Admission by appointment).
This small temple (second century) located in the ancient Forum Boarium (the cattle market) was consecrated as a church in the ninth century and still contains frescoes from that time. During the Renaissance the church was modernized, but in 1925 it was restored to its original antique appearance (by Antonio Muñoz).

⓰ Santa Maria Maggiore, pp. 22, 29, 45–48, 59, 204, 221 [16]
One of Rome's seven pilgrim churches. Santa Maria Maggiore was erected during the reign of Pope Sixtus III (432–440), whose pontificate also saw the building of the Lateran Baptistery ❶ and San Pietro in Vincoli [15] as well, possibly, as the completion of Santa Sabina ❿. It contains a uniform collection of marble columns with Ionic capitals, but these are in fact the result of a restoration in the eighteenth century. During this restoration

Other noteworthy spolia churches

the original, more diverse Ionic capitals and bases of standard Early Christian manufacture were replaced and the column shafts all altered to the same style in polished, pale-grey *Proconnesian* marble [17]. In the Early Christian church six of the then twenty (two more were added later) shafts were of coarse, green-veined *cipollino*. On the wall of the *triumphal arch* in the nave and above the entablature on the wall of the *clerestory* one can still see the original mosaics from the time of Sixtus III. In the apse is a magnificent mosaic by Jacopo Torriti (1295).

17 Santa Maria Rotonda or **Santa Maria ad Martyres** (Pantheon), pp. 19, 52–56, 61, 78 [20]
This temple, built by the Emperor Hadrian (118–125) was consecrated as a church under Pope Boniface IV (608–615) after the building was handed over to him by the Byzantine Emperor Phocas. This is the earliest definite record we find in Rome of a temple being converted into a church. In 663 the Byzantine Emperor Constans II had the dome's bronze covering removed and transported to Byzantium. In 1626 Pope Urban VIII, a member of the Barberini family, ordered the bronze ceiling of the *portico* to be melted down and the metal used to cast canons for the Castel Sant'Angelo. This pillaging of the building prompted the wry saying "Quod non fecerunt barbari, fecerunt Barberini" – What the barbarians didn't do, the Barberini did. It was also in the 1620s that the building was 'Christianized' by the addition of two towers (often credited to G. L. Bernini, but probably the work of architects Carlo Maderno and Francesco Borromini) [20]. These towers were removed in the nineteenth century.

8 Santa Maria in Trastevere, pp. 57, 59, 65, **174–183**

18 San Martino ai Monti, pp. 50, 59
This ninth-century church replaced a church from the early fifth century which may have been built on top of an older *titulus*. It sits on top of an Ancient Roman building which is open to visitors (Thurs. 9.15 a.m.–11.00 a.m.). The church's ninth-century interior was modernized in the mid-seventeenth century, but the nave is still lined on either side by twelve fine columns of pale- and dark-grey marble. Of the capitals in the two colonnades the first four pairs from the entrance are Composite, the rest are Corinthian; some have been restored in the seventeenth century using stucco and the pairs around the *presbytery* have

Other noteworthy spolia churches

been gilded. The bases (the first three of white marble, the rest dark-grey) and the *plinths* are of different styles, but have been greatly restored. At either end of the left side-aisle are frescoes of church interiors painted by Filippo Gagliardi (1648–1649), the architect responsible for the restoration of San Martino. One of these frescoes shows Gagliardi's rough reconstruction of how the Lateran Basilica, which was being modernized at that time by Borromini, might have looked in its Early Christian form [4]; the other presents a somewhat less reliable depiction of the old St Peter's (the demolition of which was completed half a century earlier).

19 **Santi Nereo e Achilleo** in the Catacombs of Domitilla, p. 49
This church, which lies partially underground, was built in the late fourth century on the site of an underground cemetery (*catacombs*). The building, which collapsed and was buried in the ninth century, probably due to an earthquake, was rediscovered in the 1870s, excavated and rebuilt. Two spolia columns from the *narthex* of the original basilica have survived, along with four spolia columns of different materials from either side of this triple-naved church. Gone now are the galleries which Santi Nereo e Achilleo also originally contained, similar to those seen in the catacomb churches of San Lorenzo fuori le Mura **6** and Sant'Agnese fuori le Mura **2**.

9 **San Nicola in Carcere**, pp. 37, 56, 66, **184–193**

20 **San Paolo fuori le Mura**, pp. 29–30, 40–41, 48, 59, 221 [13] [14] [27]
This large and impressive Early Christian basilica with the twenty columns running down either side of its nave was erected in the 380s. It burned down in 1823 and was then rebuilt. The remains of the original capitals and bases and fragments of columns are displayed in the so-called 'Passegiata archeologica' alongside the church. These testify to the wide diversity of elements which the old church contained, even though a stonemason's workshop was erected on the site during its construction for the fashioning of the imported raw materials, as had previously been the custom. By this time, however, it was no longer common for elements to be 'tailored' in such a way for a building on this scale. Interestingly, despite the availability of newly produced pieces, the builders chose to use a wide variety

Other noteworthy spolia churches

of architectural elements, something which suggests that they found the variation normally offered by the use of spolia aesthetically and architecturally appealing.

Be sure also to visit the very beautiful cloister from around 1200 with its *Cosmatesque* mosaics.

㉑ St Peter's (San Pietro), pp. 27, 29–32, 41, 59, 61–63, 221 [**11**] [**23**]
St Peter's, the papal seat, was built on the site of a Roman necropolis and – tradition has it – over the tomb of St Peter himself. The Early Christian basilica which was erected here in the fourth century was demolished in the sixteenth-seventeenth centuries and replaced by the present church. It had always been assumed that it was founded by the Emperor Constantine, a fact which was obviously of great ecclesiastical significance since he is considered to be the first Christian emperor. Recent research suggests, however, that the church was not built until after his death by one of his sons (mid-fourth century).

The Early Christian church contained a varied collection of spolia columns which in Renaissance times were generally believed to have come from the mausoleum of the Emperor Hadrian (Castel Sant'Angelo). The modern church also boasts columns and decorations in a rich and colourful variety of marbles, but here the various elements have been adapted and modernized to the point where they are no longer recognizable as spolia. One series of white, spiral Composite columns – Greek spolia used in the Early Christian church – now frames the balconies above the crossing in the church.

San Pietro: see ㉑ St Peter's

㉒ San Pietro in Vincoli, pp. 44–45, 59, 204 [**15**]
This church from the reign of Pope Sixtus III (432–440) was founded with imperial support. The chancel was modernized during the sixteenth century and the nave was furnished with a new barrel-vaulted ceiling at the beginning of the eighteenth century. The spolia colonnades lining the nave are quite unique, consisting as they do of twenty identical columns (ten on each side) with *fluted* shafts of *Proconnesian* marble and matching bases and capitals (first century) – and of the seldom employed Doric order at that. Instead of carrying the entablature which they doubtless supported in their original location these columns have, however, been combined with arcades. A similar break with classical uniformity can be seen in the *triumphal arch* whose

columns differ in stone and style from those in the nave: these being of grey granite with Byzantine Corinthian capitals, probably dating from around the time of the church's construction. The church is famous for its marble statue of Moses executed by Michelangelo (around 1514) for the tomb of Pope Julius II.

23 Santa Prassede, p. 78 [**30**]–[**35**]

This most noteworthy church dates back to Early Christian times, but was renovated during the reign of the Emperor Hadrian I (772–795) and totally rebuilt by Pope Paschal I (817–824), at which time it acquired its present form. Today, the church is entered from the Via di Santa Prassede, but the original entrance is on the Via di San Martino ai Monti. This has a porch (thirteenth century) which gave onto the *atrium* of the church. It consists of two granite columns with bases made from inverted Doric spolia capitals which have been cut to fit [**30**]. The columns support Ionic capitals, the right one of ancient origin, the left medieval.

The interior of Paschal I's church was furnished with granite spolia columns and its double triumphal arch and *apse* decorated with exquisite mosaics [**33**]. Three of the original eleven columns in each colonnade were later bricked up inside piers in order to strengthen the church's structure, with the result that only eight columns on either side are now visible. At the end of each side-aisle other spolia columns support an entablature. The church underwent a process of modernization from the latter half of the sixteenth century to around 1600, during which the diverse spolia capitals and entablatures were rendered more uniform in appearance with the aid of stucco. In more recent times the stucco has been removed here and there, revealing the original (very varied) elements [**34**] [**35**]. The floor is a reproduction from around 1918 of the Roman *Cosmatesque* style (by Antonio Muñoz). Note also the distinctive Roman leaf-covered columns in white marble set into the wall on either side of the *presbytery*. These columns were discovered in 1729 and placed in their current positions at that time.

Santa Prassede also houses the Chapel of San Zeno (this too from the time of Paschal I) whose entrance is framed by a mix of ancient spolia (including shafts of black *porphyry* and an entablature from the third century) and elements produced in the ninth century (including column bases and ionic capitals) [**31**]

[**32**]. The dome of the chapel is borne up by two pairs of spolia columns; one of these (to the right of the altar) is set on a *plinth* dating from the fifth-sixth century and combined with an inverted late-antique capital employed as an extra high base to compensate for the short shaft. The other three stand on ninth-century replicas of the first plinth. The wall above the entrance to the chapel and the chapel dome are decorated with extraordinarily beautiful mosaics. On display next to the Chapel of San Zeno is the church's greatest relic – both in sacred and architectural terms: a piece of the column to which Christ was bound and flagellated.

24 Santa Prisca, p. 51

This church, whose history can be traced back to an Early Christian *titulus*, acquired its essential form under Pope Adrian I (722–795) but has been restored and rebuilt several times since then. Now only the shafts of the original colonnades (of various sorts of grey marble and grey granite) are visible, partly embedded as they were inside piers in the eighteenth century. The church was erected on top of a Roman house containing a *mithraeum* (second century) (viewing by appointment only, second and fourth Saturdays of each month).

25 Santa Pudenziana, p. 50

This church dates back to the end of the fourth century, but it was modernized in the late sixteenth century at which time the two rows of spolia columns in the nave were bricked up inside piers. The chancel was remodelled at the beginning of the nineteenth century, but the splendid fifth-century *apse* mosaic was left untouched. Santa Pudenziana is built on top of an Ancient Roman house which is open to visitors.

26 Santi Quattro Coronati

This church lies in a peaceful, almost country-like spot on top of a hill, only a few steps from San Clemente **3** and the crowds of tourists around the Colosseum. Its history can be traced back to a sixth-century *titulus* which was replaced by a church during the reign of Pope Honorius I (625–638). This church was in turn renovated by Leo IV (847–855). Later, under Paschal II (1099–1118) and after having suffering damage in the sack of Rome by the Normans in 1084, it was rebuilt in a somewhat reduced form. Numerous renovations and rebuildings have resulted in a fascinating building boasting a rich variety of spolia and many visible historical layers. In the body of the church is a lovely twelfth-century *Cosmatesque* floor inlaid with a number of marble spolia tiles bearing inscriptions (see p. 2). Set into the wall on the right-hand side of the courtyard in front of the church and in the right-hand wall inside Santi Quattro Coronati is an older row of columns, once the right-hand colonnade of the church, before Paschal had it reduced in breadth and in length. The church was subsequently taken over by Benedictine monks who added a cloister to the building. Still later the monastery passed into the hands of Augustinian nuns and is still home to this order. Be sure also to visit the adjoining Chapel of St Sylvester with its beautiful, well-preserved frescoes from the mid-thirteenth century, splendid Cosmatesque floor (entrance on the right side of the courtyard in front of the church) and the simple, tranquil early thirteenth-century cloister (entrance from the church's left side-aisle).

27 San Saba

Originally the oratory of a seventh-century monastery (established within an Ancient Roman house) San Saba was converted into a triple-naved basilica probably sometime in the mid-twelfth century and renovated around 1205. The church underwent major restoration (including the relaying of the thirteenth-century *Cosmatesque* floor) in the early 1930s and now looks more or less as it would have done in the twelfth century. Embedded in the wall of the *portico* are ancient inscriptions, gravestones and the like. This lovely and quietly atmospheric church, which lies in a secluded spot in a leafy residential area, contains a very varied selection of spolia columns with granite and marble shafts, mostly topped by Ionic *impost capitals*, though with one Composite and one Corinthian capital at the beginning and end of the left-hand colonnade. Note also the bases in different styles and sizes, not least the green *porphyry* (serpentine) bases supporting the first pair of columns. A rather unusual feature on the left side of the church is the additional little side-aisle, supported by one smooth and two *half-fluted*, short marble columns without capitals. In a corresponding, but enclosed area on the right side of the church are another two columns. The *ciborium* is a modern reconstruction and includes two unusual Composite capitals in green porphyry.

⑩ Santa Sabina, pp. 44–45, 59, 74, 127, **194–205**, 212

㉘ Sancta Sanctorum

(9.30 a.m.–12.40 a.m. and 3.30 p.m.–4.00 p.m., Closed Sundays and holidays)

This sumptuously decorated building, which has been the Pope's private chapel since Early Christian times and contains a priceless collection of relics, lies at the top of the so-called Scala Santa (Holy Stairs). Legend has it that this is a flight of spolia steps from the palace of Pontius Pilate in Jerusalem – the self-same ones that Christ climbed when brought before Pilate prior to his crucifixion. It is said that Helena, the mother of the Emperor Constantine had the steps sent to Rome in the fourth century. Nowadays pilgrims climb them on their knees. Other visitors can use the ordinary flights of steps on either side of the holy stairs. On the landing at the top are three marble spolia doorways, also imported from Jerusalem. In its present form the chapel dates from the reign of Pope Nicholas III (1277–1280). The small *presbytery* and its altar are separated from the lofty main chamber by two splendid *porphyry* columns with gilded Composite capitals on which rests an entablature decorated with *Cosmatesque* mosaics. The walls are clad in panels of porphyry and grey-striped and purple-veined *pavonazzetto*. The presbytery ceiling is decorated with mosaics and the upper walls and ceiling in the chapel are adorned with frescoes from the late sixteenth and thirteenth centuries respectively. The floor is laid with fine Cosmatesque work.

⑪ Santo Stefano Rotondo, pp. 22, 51, 65, 76, 183, 204, **206–217**

Temple of Antoninus and Faustina: see San Lorenzo in Miranda

Popes mentioned in this book

88–97	Clemens I
422–432	Celestine I
432–440	Sixtus III
440–461	Leo I (the Great)
461–468	Hilary
468–483	Simplicius
526–530	Felix IV
578–590	Pelagius II
590–604	Gregor I (the Great)
608–615	Bonifacius IV
625–638	Honorius I
640–642	John IV
642–649	Theodor
772–795	Hadrian I
817–824	Paschalis I
847–855	Leo IV
858–867	Nicolaus I
872–882	John VIII
1088–1099	Urban II
1099–1118	Paschalis II
1118–1119	Gelasius II
1119–1124	Calixtus II
1130–1143	Innocens II
1216–1227	Honorius III
1277–1280	Nicolaus III
1305–1314	Clemens V
1447–1455	Nicolaus V
1503–1513	Julius II
1623–1644	Urban VIII
1655–1667	Alexander VII
1846–1878	Pius IX

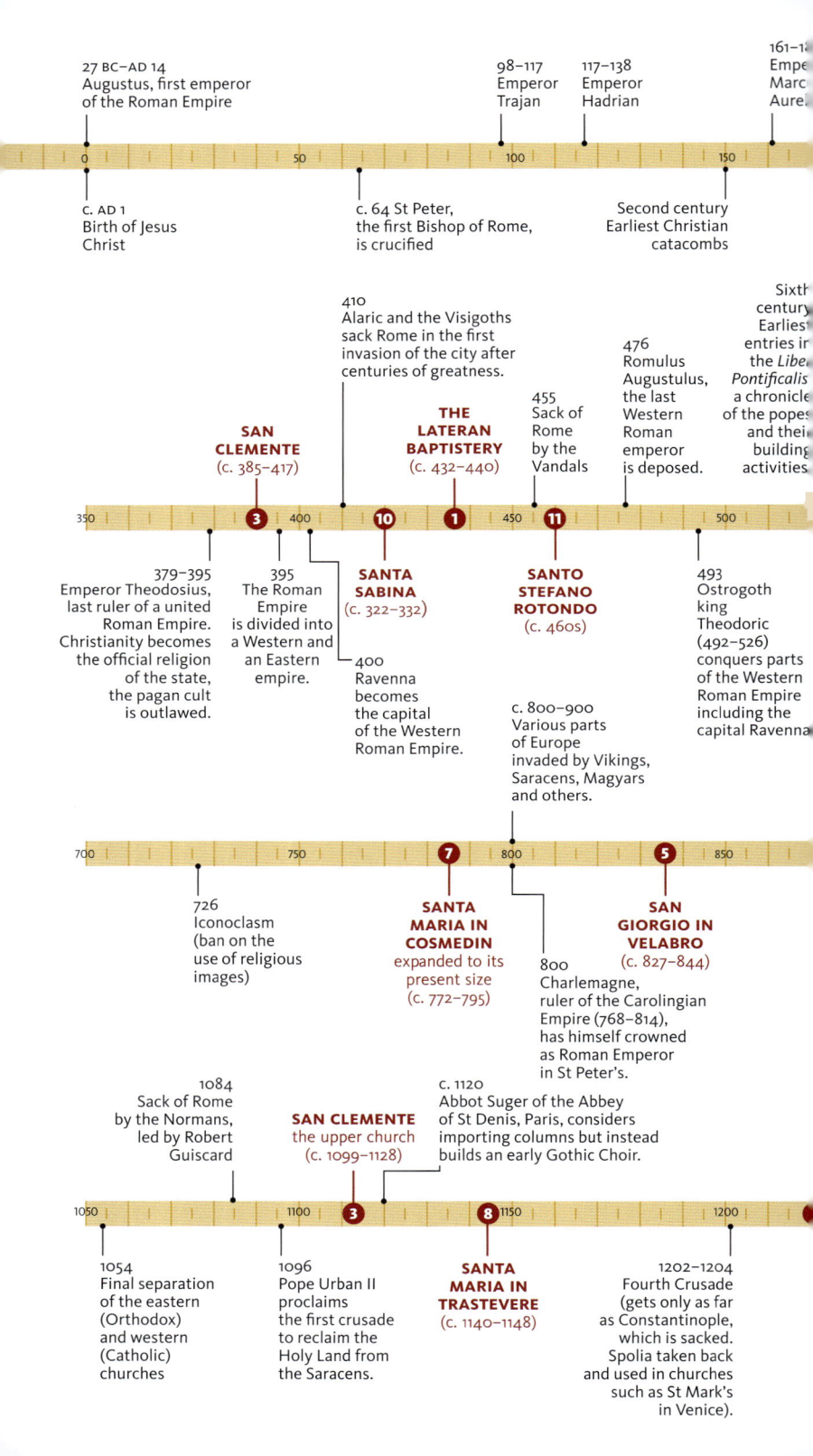

27 BC–AD 14
Augustus, first emperor of the Roman Empire

98–117
Emperor Trajan

117–138
Emperor Hadrian

161–1[...]
Empe[...]
Marc[...]
Aure[...]

| 0 | | | | | 50 | | | | | 100 | | | | | 150 | | |

c. AD 1
Birth of Jesus Christ

c. 64 St Peter, the first Bishop of Rome, is crucified

Second century
Earliest Christian catacombs

410
Alaric and the Visigoths sack Rome in the first invasion of the city after centuries of greatness.

THE LATERAN BAPTISTERY
(c. 432–440)

455
Sack of Rome by the Vandals

476
Romulus Augustulus, the last Western Roman emperor is deposed.

Sixth century
Earlies[...] entries in the *Libe[...] Pontificalis* a chronicle of the popes and their building activities[...]

SAN CLEMENTE
(c. 385–417)

| 350 | | | | ③ | 400 | | | ⑩ | | ① | | 450 | ⑪ | | | | | 500 | |

379–395
Emperor Theodosius, last ruler of a united Roman Empire. Christianity becomes the official religion of the state, the pagan cult is outlawed.

395
The Roman Empire is divided into a Western and an Eastern empire.

SANTA SABINA
(c. 322–332)

400
Ravenna becomes the capital of the Western Roman Empire.

SANTO STEFANO ROTONDO
(c. 460s)

493
Ostrogoth king Theodoric (492–526) conquers parts of the Western Roman Empire including the capital Ravenna

---

c. 800–900
Various parts of Europe invaded by Vikings, Saracens, Magyars and others.

| 700 | | | | | 750 | | | ⑦ | | | 800 | | | | ⑤ | 850 | |

726
Iconoclasm (ban on the use of religious images)

SANTA MARIA IN COSMEDIN
expanded to its present size
(c. 772–795)

800
Charlemagne, ruler of the Carolingian Empire (768–814), has himself crowned as Roman Emperor in St Peter's.

SAN GIORGIO IN VELABRO
(c. 827–844)

1084
Sack of Rome by the Normans, led by Robert Guiscard

SAN CLEMENTE
the upper church
(c. 1099–1128)

c. 1120
Abbot Suger of the Abbey of St Denis, Paris, considers importing columns but instead builds an early Gothic Choir.

| 1050 | | | | | 1100 | | ③ | | | ⑧ | 1150 | | | | | 1200 | | ● |

1054
Final separation of the eastern (Orthodox) and western (Catholic) churches

1096
Pope Urban II proclaims the first crusade to reclaim the Holy Land from the Saracens.

SANTA MARIA IN TRASTEVERE
(c. 1140–1148)

1202–1204
Fourth Crusade (gets only as far as Constantinople, which is sacked. Spolia taken back and used in churches such as St Mark's in Venice).

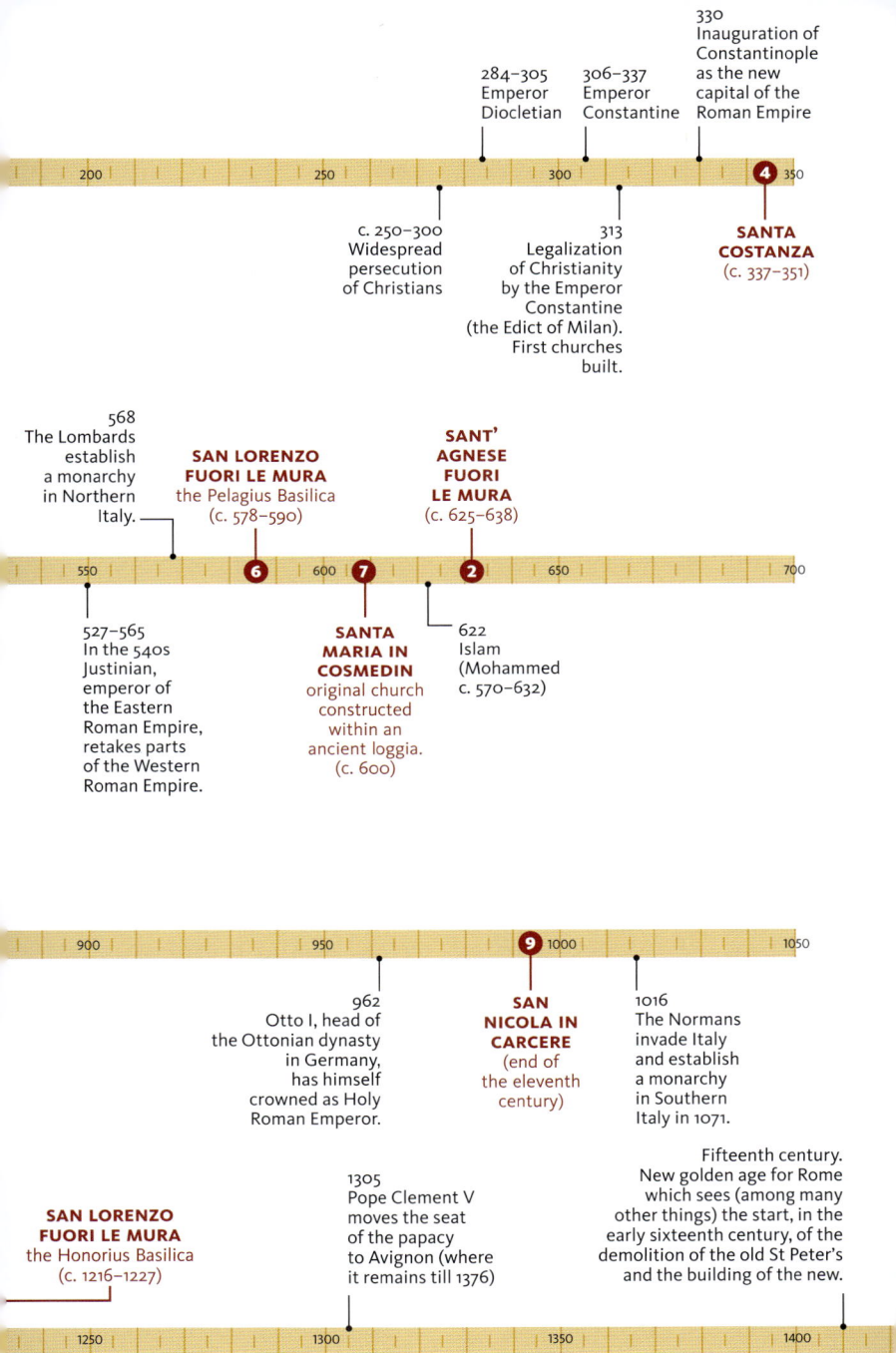

284–305
Emperor
Diocletian

306–337
Emperor
Constantine

330
Inauguration of
Constantinople
as the new
capital of the
Roman Empire

❹ 350

200 | 250 | 300

**SANTA
COSTANZA**
(c. 337–351)

c. 250–300
Widespread
persecution
of Christians

313
Legalization
of Christianity
by the Emperor
Constantine
(the Edict of Milan).
First churches
built.

568
The Lombards
establish
a monarchy
in Northern
Italy.

**SAN LORENZO
FUORI LE MURA**
the Pelagius Basilica
(c. 578–590)

**SANT'
AGNESE
FUORI
LE MURA**
(c. 625–638)

550 | ❻ 600 | ❼ | ❷ | 650 | 700

527–565
In the 540s
Justinian,
emperor of
the Eastern
Roman Empire,
retakes parts
of the Western
Roman Empire.

**SANTA
MARIA IN
COSMEDIN**
original church
constructed
within an
ancient loggia.
(c. 600)

622
Islam
(Mohammed
c. 570–632)

---

900 | 950 | ❾ 1000 | 1050

962
Otto I, head of
the Ottonian dynasty
in Germany,
has himself
crowned as Holy
Roman Emperor.

**SAN
NICOLA IN
CARCERE**
(end of
the eleventh
century)

1016
The Normans
invade Italy
and establish
a monarchy
in Southern
Italy in 1071.

Fifteenth century.
New golden age for Rome
which sees (among many
other things) the start, in the
early sixteenth century, of the
demolition of the old St Peter's
and the building of the new.

1305
Pope Clement V
moves the seat
of the papacy
to Avignon (where
it remains till 1376)

**SAN LORENZO
FUORI LE MURA**
the Honorius Basilica
(c. 1216–1227)

1250 | 1300 | 1350 | 1400

Timeline

Setting a selection of historical events
and figures and the eleven selected spolia churches
into their historical context.

Glossary

Specialist terms are given in italics the first time they are mentioned in the introductory chapters or in the descriptions of churches.

acanthus [**111**]: plant with large, jagged leaves. The stylized leaf motif used on Corinthian *capitals* was inspired by the acanthus plant. The acanthus also crops up in ornamental form in Early Christian and medieval art, e.g. in church *apse* mosaics [**55**].

ad corpus: term used of a church (or, more specifically, the altar of a church) built directly over the grave or tomb of a saint.

ambulatory [**61**]: a semi-circular aisle running around a central space.

apse [**66**] [**99**]: a semi-circular or domed structure situated at the end of the chancel or *presbytery*, or a chapel in a church.

architrave: see *entablature*

atrium: a court, often colonnaded, in front of a church. The only well-preserved medieval atrium in Rome is that of San Clemente [**55**].

baldachin: see *ciborium*

basilica (pp. 28–29) [**11**] [**99**]: a Roman building used for courts of law and public assemblies. In the fourth century this style of building was adopted for churches. The basilica was a large, oblong hall ending in a *presbytery* with a semicircular *apse*. It was often entered by way of a vestibule or *narthex*. The central section of the hall, the nave, was usually flanked by two or four lower side-aisles and sometimes a transept, giving the building a cruciform shape – an obviously symbolic factor for a Christian congregation. The aisles were normally separated by colonnades and the walls of the nave furnished with windows (the *clerestory*).

campanile (pp. 162–163): church bell-tower.

capital: the topmost member of a column, the column's 'head'. In Roman times the main types of capital used were those of the Ionic [**89**], Doric (less common) [**15**], Corinthian and *Composite* [**65**] orders, which is to say: capitals, shafts, bases and *entablatures* adhering to particular sets of proportions and styles of ornamentation [**12**]. But there are many different variants of the classical capitals, including figural capitals carved with reliefs of various sorts [**72**] or full-leaf Corinthian or Composite capitals carved with simplified versions of the traditional elaborate, naturalistic *acanthus* leaves [**106**]. While the Ionic, Doric and Corinthian styles are of Greek origin, the Composite order was not invented until the time of the Roman Empire. The Composite order combines two of the Greek

111 Acanthus

prototypes, the Ionic and the Corinthian, in one capital. See *column orders*; see *Composite*

catacombs: the Early Christian subterranean cemeteries of Rome, with tombs dug out of the local *tufa* bedrock. This practice of burying the dead replaced the Roman custom of cremation, since Christians believed that on the Day of Judgement the dead would be physically resurrected. The catacombs are labyrinthine networks of passages, level upon level reaching far underground. In a few cases they also contain small chapel-like chambers or basilicas, like Santi Nereo e Achilleo in the Domitilla catacombs (*20*) with its fine varied selection of *spolia*. The widespread legend that persecuted Christians sought refuge in the catacombs during the third century has proved to have no basis in fact.

cella: the windowless inner chamber of a Roman temple housing the cult image. Laymen were not allowed to enter the cella, only the priests; public sacrifices were conducted outdoors in front of the temple [**91**].

ciborium [**70**]: a column-borne canopy or baldachin covering the high altar in the chancel or *presbytery* of a church

clerestory/clerestory walls: the side walls pierced with windows above the *colonnades* on either side of the nave [**99**].

colonnade: a row of columns

column order [**12**]: the system of architectural elements: column bases, shafts, *capitals* and *entablatures* with their corresponding proportions and ornamentation. Developed in Ancient Greece and adopted by the Ancient Romans. The main types used by the Romans were the Doric (though this was less common), Ionic, Corinthian and *Composite*.

Composite: Roman style of capital in which the acanthus leaves of the Corinthian capital are combined with the volutes and egg-and-dart frieze of the Ionic [**37**]. Can be seen as an example of the general Roman strategy of appropriating elements of conquered civilizations and blending them together to form new styles. The Composite order was used, most aptly, in Roman

Glossary

240

triumphal arches (though not in the Arch of Constantine), but was (understandably) never particularly popular in the Eastern Greek, or Byzantine, part of the Roman Empire.

corbel: a projection or bracket of stone, timber etc., jutting out from a wall to support weight.

Corinthian: see *capital*

Cosmatesque [80]: term used of a style of ornamental marble inlays and mosaics, used primarily on the floors and marble furniture in churches. The name derives from the Cosmati family who had one of the leading marble workshops in the Roman area in the thirteenth century. But the term 'Cosmatesque' is also used more generally to describe stone inlay work from countless other workshops. This style of decoration was common in the twelfth and thirteenth centuries. The combination of small mosaic blocks ('tesserae') and *opus sectile* was used to create complex geometric patterns. The rectangular and circular tiles were cut out of pieces of *spolia* marble of all sorts (columns, tiles, revetments etc.) and colours: red and green *porphyry* (serpentine), *giallo antico*, *pavonazzetto* and so on. The large, circular tiles (*rotae*) in the floor are slices cut from *spolia* columns. This kind of floor inlay is sometimes also called *opus alexandrinum*.

domus ecclesiae: A domus is a Roman house. Before the building of churches was legalized by the Emperor Constantine in the early fourth century, Christian congregations met in ordinary houses which were owned by Christians and were big enough to house the congregation; these house churches were known as domus ecclesiae.

Doric: see *capital*

Early Christian: term used to describe the first centuries of Christian history, a period which gradually passed into the Early Middle Ages. The terms 'Late Antiquity' and 'Early Medieval' are largely synonymous; which one is used depends mostly on whether the focus is on the traditions of Ancient Rome or the new Christian culture. Historians differ widely in their dates for the beginning and end of the period, but in this book these are taken to be from around 300 to around 500.

entablature [12] [37]: the horizontal superstructure supported by columns in the classical Greek and Roman system of *column orders*. Consists of an *architrave*, *frieze* and *cornice*.

fascia: a horizontal ornamental band as used esp. in an *architrave*.

fluting [71]: Shallow, concave grooves cut down the length of a column, pilaster or moulding. Known from Ancient Greece and Rome. Variations of this are *spiral fluting*, in which the grooves are cut to spiral down a column, and *half-fluting*, in which grooves are cut only in the top two-thirds of the column.

funerary basilica: a particular form of Early Christian *basilica*. A U-shaped building with a covered, colonnaded *ambulatory*

Glossary

surrounding a large burial site. The well-preserved U-shaped wall from an early funerary basilica (fourth century) can be seen at Santa Costanza/Sant'Agnese [**60**].

Several other such examples from this period did exist, among them the so-called Basilica Maior (now known only from excavations of its foundations), located near San Lorenzo fuori le Mura **6** (p. 148).

gallery: see *matronei*

half-fluting [**99**]: see *fluting*.

impost (capital or block) [**51**]: Eastern Roman/Byzantine architectural element in the shape of a marble block inserted between the *capital* and the foot of the arch which the capital supports.

Ionic: see *capital*

lintel: a horizontal support across the top of a door, window or other opening.

liturgy: prescribed form or set of forms for public religious worship.

loggia: a gallery or arcade having one or both of its sides open to the air. See also *portico*.

matronei [51]: modern Italian term for the galleries found in some churches. Although the name suggests that these galleries were intended for female worshippers there is no historical evidence to support this idea. Such galleries were in fact meant to make it easier for pilgrims to view and to circulate around the saint's tomb down in the body of the church.

mithraeum [**53**]: a 'sanctuary' for the worship of the Persian sun god Mithras.

narthex [**39**]: vestibule or entrance hall with arcades leading into the nave/naves of a church.

nymphaeum: a Roman grotto or shrine dedicated to a nymph or nymphs, usually containing a fountain or well.

opus alexandrinum: see *Cosmatesque*

opus sectile [**38**] [**101**]: floor or wall decoration in which tiles – of, for example, white and grey marble or red and green *porphyry* – are laid in geometric patterns. The tiles are usually cut from pieces of *spolia*. Floor decorations of this sort from the twelfth-thirteenth centuries are generally referred to as *Cosmatesque*.

pergola [**80**]: a rood-screen or arrangement of columns separating the *presbytery* of a church (reserved for the clergy) from the rest of the nave.

plinth [**71**]: square stone slab or block on which to place a column base or sculpture. In the Middle Ages the difference in the lengths of columns was evened out by placing their bases on plinths of appropriate heights.

portico (pp. 136–137): a formal entrance to a classical temple, church or other building; open-sided, with columns at regular intervals supporting a roof.

presbytery: part of a church near the altar, reserved for the clergy.

rota [**80**]: a roundel or circular tile, often of red or green *porphyry*, inlaid in a *Cosmatesque* floor. Rotae are usually slices taken from *spolia* column shafts.

schola cantorum [**80**]: a special area of the nave of a church, closest to the *presbytery*, screened off by marble panels and reserved for the clergy or the choir.

sectile tessellato 59 [**78**]: floor decoration consisting of patterns created out of small, square tiles or mosaic blocks ('tesserae') in different coloured stones.

soffit [**98**]: the underside of a marble *entablature*, carved with a simple relief which forms a framework of sorts around the capitals supporting it.

spiral fluting: see *fluting*

spolia [**6**] [**28**] [**84**]: from the Latin 'spolium' meaning the flayed skin of an animal. In its plural form 'spolia' has come to mean the spoils of war and other kinds of plunder, including works of art. In art history spolia is a term used for architectural elements or sculptures taken from one location and placed in a new setting. In Late Antiquity, when builders first began to make serious use of spolia, the preferred, positive term for this sort of recycling was 'rediviva saxa' – 'reborn stones'.

tambour: a wall of circular plan, supporting a dome or possibly a conical roof.

thermae: Roman bath-houses.

titulus (pl. tituli): term used of Early Christian congregations and the buildings in which they met. These buildings took their 'title' from the name of the owner or founder.

trabeation: horizontal superstructure supported by columns. See *column order*, see *entablature*.

triumphal arch: Roman monument usually built to commemorate a military victory on the part of the emperor [**6**]. With the advent of Christianity the term was adopted by the Church and used of the monumental arch separating the *apse* from the nave [**18**]. In this new setting it was not, of course, a symbol of military victory, but of the triumph over death through the Christian faith. Written sources document this use of the term in the ninth century, but the placing of *capitals* bearing trophy reliefs (taken from a Roman victory monument) on either side of this arch in San Lorenzo fuori le Mura in the late sixth century suggests that the arch was associated with the triumphal motif from a much earlier date [**49**]. The citizens of Rome must have made this same association, since they employed the distinctly Roman *Composite* column order in their triumphal arches (with the Arch of Constantine as the one exception) as an allusion to the triumph of the Roman Empire over other civilizations.

Materials

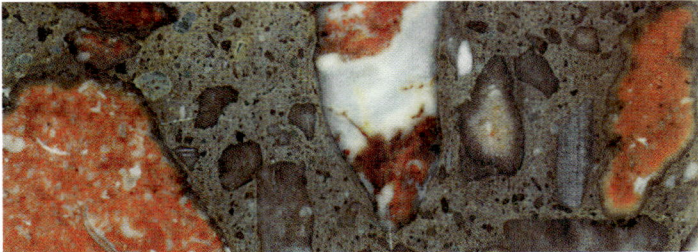

africano: colourful marble, its black ground patched with red, beige, white and grey.

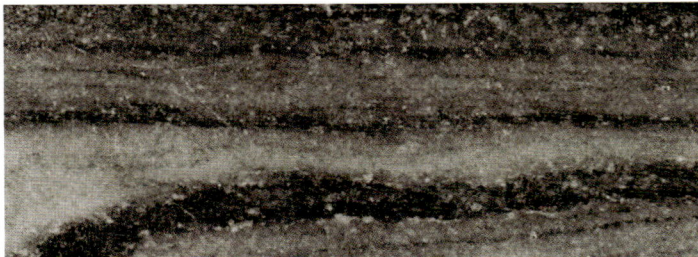

cipollino: coarse, grey-green marble with a distinctive pattern of wavy lines and concentric swirls built up from layers of green and grey mica, hence the name (from the Italian 'cipollo' meaning onion) [21].

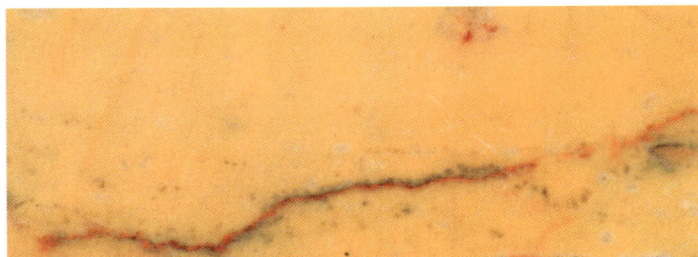

giallo antico: yellow marble [6] [26].

granite, grey: grey speckled rock found in most parts of the world in lighter or darker shades [**64**]. Roman varieties include the dark-grey *granito del Foro* and the pale-grey *granito della Troade*.

granite, red: red speckled rock from Aswan, Egypt [**64**].

pavonazzetto: white marble with lilac or purple veins [**70**].

peperino: grey *tufa*. Coarse, porous, cement-like volcanic rock. Was usually faced with stucco (pp. 184–185).

porphyry, red: purplish-red, speckled ('phenocryst') rock from Egypt's 'Mons Porphyrites' [26] [36].

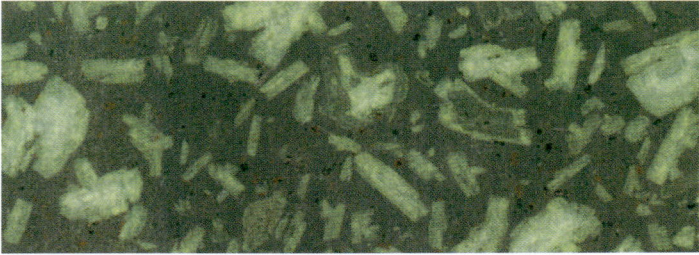

porphyry, green (serpentin): dark-green rock with paler spots ('phenocryst') or small, rectangular patches [26] [45].

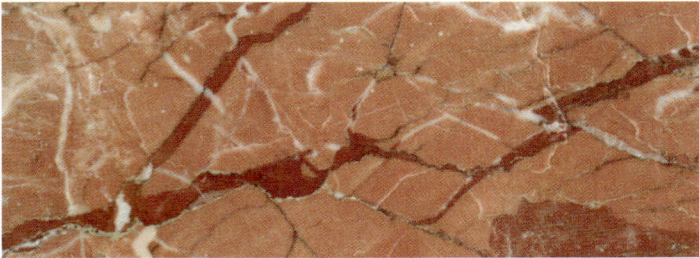

portasanta: red marble with grey/brown/white veins [49].

Proconnesian: evenly coloured white- and grey-striped marble (from what is now Turkey) [15].

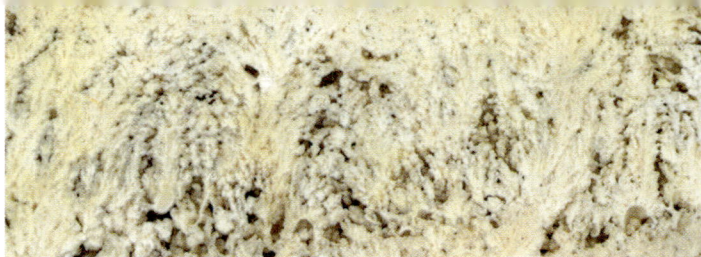

travertine: cream-coloured limestone, porous and dotted with small holes [**85**].

tufa: reddish-brown, porous volcanic rock [**85**].

verde antico: green-mottled marble [**5**].

Bibliography

For full bibliographical details of the many books and articles used as sources for this work and to which I am indebted please see my book: *The Eloquence of Appropriation. Prolegomena to an Understanding of Spolia in Early Christian Rome* (Analecta Romana Instituti Danici, Supplementum XXXIII), 'L'Erma' di Bretschneider, Rome, 2003.

For a recent, well-illustrated guide to early Roman churches – up to the seventh century – (also containing details of bibliographic sources) see H. Brandenburg: *Die frühchristlichen Kirchen Roms* von 4. bis zum 7. Jahrhundert. Der beginn der abendländischen Kirchenbaukunst, Schnell & Steiner, 2004. This is also available in English and Italian translations.

A well-illustrated guide to the churches of Rome from earliest times to the present day (with particular emphasis on the use of spolia) can be found in R. Bernabei: *Chiese di Roma*, Electa, 2007.

An important analysis of the history and meaning of columns from Antiquity to the Renaissance is provided by J. Onians: *Bearers of Meaning. The Classical Orders in Antiquity, the Middle Ages and the Renaissance*, Princeton University Press, 1988.

Index

Words in *italics* are mentioned in the Glossary (p. 238)
or the section on Materials (p. 243); names given in **bold** indicate
churches described and illustrated in the sections on 'Selected
spolia churches' or 'Other noteworthy spolia churches'.

Photo credits

Camilla Borghese, Rome
ill. 55 © Basilica di San Clemente
ill. 87–90

Deutsches Archäologisches Institut, Rome
ill. 77

Det Kongelige Bibliotek, Copenhagen
ill. 20

Maria Fabricius Hansen, Copenhagen
ill. 1, 2, 3, 7, 9, 22, 24, 28, 29, 30, 43, 44, 63, 73, 111
p. 2, pp. 112–113, pp. 124–125, pp. 136–137, pp. 146–147, pp. 162–163, pp. 194–195, pp. 206–207, p. 218, p. 220

Pernille Klemp, Copenhagen
Cover illustration
ill. 5, 6, 8, 13, 14, 15, 17, 18, 19, 21, 26, 27, 31, 32, 33, 34, 35, 36, 37, 40, 41, 42, 45, 47, 49, 50, 51, 54, 56, 57, 58, 59, 61, 64, 65, 67, 68, 69, 70, 71, 72, 74, 75, 78, 80, 81, 82, 83, 84, 86, 92, 94, 95, 96, 97, 98, 99, 100, 101, 103, 104, 106, 107, 108, 109, 110
p. 6 and p. 8 (detail of ill. 26), p. 84 (detail of ill. 78) pp. 86–87, pp. 100–101, pp. 174–175, pp. 184–185

Vasari, Rome
ill. 16

Arnaldo Vescovo, Rome
ill. 38, 46, 60

Line drawings by architect Pauline Ringsted
ill. 39: Based on Giovenale, G.B.: *Il Battistero Lateranense nelle recenti indagini della Pont. Commissione di Archeologia Sacra* (Studie di antichità cristiana, I), Rome, 1929, plate I.

ill. 48; ill. 66: Based on Krautheimer, R. (et al.): *Corpus Basilicarum Christianarum Romae. The Early Christian Basilicas of Rome*, Città del Vaticano, 1937–1977, I, Plates IV & VI, 1; I, Plate XXXIII.
ill. 62: Based on Wilson Jones, M.: *Principles of Roman Architecture*, New Haven & London 2000, fig. 4. 11.
ill. 88: Based on Bunsen, C.C.J.: *Die Basiliken des christlichen Roms nach ihrem Zusammenhange mit Idee und Geschichte der Kirchenbaukunst*, Munich, 1842, Tafeln, XV, c.
ill. 105: Based on Ceschi, C.: *Santo Stefano Rotondo* (Atti della Pontificia Accademia Romana di Archeologia. Serie III: Memorie, XV), Rome, 1982, fig. 212.

The Spolia Churches of Rome

© Maria Fabricius Hansen and Aarhus University Press 2015
Translation copyright © Barbara J. Haveland 2015
Original title: *Genbrugskirker i Rom*, 2010

Design: Carl-H.K. Zakrisson
Cover photo (Santa Costanza): Pernille Klemp
Pictures of floor mosaics and columns used to separate chapters:
p. 2: Santi Quattro Coronati
pp. 6 & 8: San Giovanni a Porta Latina
p. 84: San Lorenzo fuori le Mura
p. 218: San Clemente, lower church
p. 220: The Lateran Baptistery
Typeset in Lexicon and Kievit
on 115gm. G-print and printed by Narayana Press

Printed in Denmark 2015

ISBN 978 87 7124 210 2

AARHUS UNIVERSITY PRESS
Langelandsgade 177, 8200 Aarhus N
www.unipress.dk

INTERNATIONAL DISTRIBUTORS:

Gazelle Book Services Ltd.
White Cross Mills, Hightown, Lancaster, LA1 4XS, United Kingdom
www.gazellebookservices.co.uk

IS Distribution
70 Enterprise Drive, Suite 2, Bristol, CT 06010 USA
www.isdistribution.com

The publication of this book was made possible by grants from:
The Augustinus Foundation
Beckett-Fonden
C.L. Davids Fond
Margot og Thorvald Dreyers Fond
Landsdommer V. Gieses Legat

Reproductions from other works

ill. 4: Grabar, A.: *The Beginnings of Christian Art 200–395*, Gilbert, S. & Emmons, J. (transl.), London, 1967, Fig. 183.

ill. 11: Rice, L.: *Altars and Altarpieces of New St. Peter's. Outfitting the Basilica, 1621–1666*, Cambridge & New York, 1997, p. 365, Fig. 16, Biblioteca Apostolica Vaticana, Barb. Lat. 2733, ff. 104–105.

ill. 12: Perrault, C.: *Ordonnance des cinq especes de colonnes selon la methode des anciens*, Paris, 1683, Planche I.

ill. 23: Bösel, R. & Frommel, C.L. (eds.): *Borromini e l'universo barocco*, Milano 2000, p. 140 (detail).

ill. 25: Kinney, D.: "Making Mute Stones Speak. Reading Columns in S. Nicola in Carcere and S.

Maria in Aracoeli", in Striker, Cecil L. (ed.): *Architectural Studies in Memory of Richard Krautheimer*, Verlag Philipp von Zabern, 1996, Plate 40, Fig. 8. Photo: Dale Kinney, reproduced by kind permission of Dale Kinney.

ill. 52: Brandenburg, H.: *Die frühchristlichen Kirchen Roms vom 4. bis zum 7. Jahrhundert. Der Beginn der abendländischen Kirchenbaukunst*, Jaca Book, Milano & Verlag Schnell und Steiner, Regensburg, 2004, II.19, Fig. XIX.4

ill. 76: Bunsen, C.C.J.: *Die Basiliken des christlichen Roms nach ihrem Zusammenhange mit Idee und Geschichte der Kirchenbaukunst*, Tafeln, Munich, 1842, detail of Plate XII

ill. 79: Krautheimer, R.: "The Crypt of Sta. Maria in Cosmedin and the Mausoleum of Probus Anicius", in Freeman Sandler, L. (ed.): *Essays in Memory of Karl Lehmann*, New York, 1964, Fig. 4.

ill. 91: Lugli, G.: *Roma antica. Il centro monumentale*, Rome, 1946, fig. 169.

ill. 102: Brandenburg, Hugo: "Die Verwendung von Spolien und originalen Werkstücken in der spätantiken Arkitektur", in Poeschke, J. (ed.): *Antike Spolien in der Architektur des Mittelalters und der Renaissance*, Munich, 1996, p. 13, Fig. 1.

pp. 243–246: Price, M.T.: *The sourcebook of decorative stone*, Firefly Books, 2007.

1. The Lateran Baptistery
2. Sant'Agnese fuori le Mura
3. San Clemente
4. Santa Costanza
5. San Giorgio in Velabro
6. San Lorenzo fuori le Mura
7. Santa Maria in Cosmedin
8. Santa Maria in Trastevere
9. San Nicola in Carcere
10. Santa Sabina
11. Santo Stefano Rotondo

1. Sant'Adriano
2. San Bartolomeo all'Isola
3. San Benedetto in Piscinula
4. Santa Bibiana
5. Santi Cosma e Damiano
6. San Crisogono
7. San Giovanni in Laterano
   (the Lateran Basilica)
8. San Giovanni a Porta Latina
9. Santi Giovanni e Paolo
10. San Lorenzo in Miranda
11. Santa Maria degli Angeli
12. Santa Maria Antiqua
13. Santa Maria in Aracoeli
14. Santa Maria in Domnica
15. Santa Maria Egiziaca
16. Santa Maria Maggiore
17. Santa Maria Rotonda
18. San Martino ai Monti
19. Santi Nereo e Achilleo
20. San Paolo fuori le Mura
21. St Peter's (San Pietro)
22. San Pietro in Vincoli
23. Santa Prassede
24. Santa Prisca
25. Santa Pudenziana
26. Santi Quattro Coronati
27. San Saba
28. Sancta Sanctorum